Johny Pierre (JEAN)
Mary Madeleine
David Daniel (Danny)
René Frederick
Fernand Patrick
Pierre Leon

THE HOUSE OF DAVID

The House of David

Marguerite Porthouse

Best wishes.
Marguerite Porthouse.

UNITED WRITERS
Cornwall

UNITED WRITERS PUBLICATIONS LTD
Ailsa, Castle Gate, Penzance, Cornwall.

All Rights Reserved. No part of this publication may be reproduced, stored in a retrieval system, or transmitted, in any form or by any means, electronic, mechanical, photocopying, recording or otherwise, without the prior permission of the Copyright owner.

British Library Cataloguing in Publication Data:
A catalogue record for this book is
available from the British Library.

ISBN 1 85200 099 6

Copyright © 2002 Marguerite Porthouse

Printed in Great Britain by
United Writers Publications Ltd
Cornwall.

To Rene-Marie
and David Docherty-Keyeux
for their bravery in saving
the lives of their family.

Preface

In 1940 I chronicled the tragic events which completely changed the lives of my family. From the little village of Andrimont, situated in the Belgian Ardennes, we fled when the German invasion started on a beautiful sunny morning on the 10th May 1940.

We were a British family. In fear of internment and worse, we had no options. I was a teenager, second eldest child in a family of ten children.

Maman wanted a record made of the incredible journey we had to make in the hope of achieving safety in England. We found out later that this tragic journey saved our lives as the Gestapo came to our village and searched for us.

My chronicle was written in French, my native tongue. In 1963 I translated my record into English but it wasn't until 1977, then involved in short story writing, that I submitted this true story to our local radio station. It was broadcast in 1978 under the title 'Escape from Belgium'. The interest in my family's tragic journey into the unknown was instant and my producer asked me to write about our lives before the horrors of war. The book *The House of David* was completed two years later. In 1986 BBC Radio Newcastle broadcast the whole story in 28 episodes. The interest in the story was wonderful, my family was very supportive and enjoyed the broadcasts and the press and media interest.

The following year the 28 episodes were repeated due to popular demand and Radio 4 awarded me the 'Best from Local Stations' award and featured some of my work.

Family commitments forced me to put away the story at this time.

Interest in *The House of David* remained, as did requests for the book. I found myself doing French translations of the work. Over the past few years extracts have been published in French for Belgian publications, and these were discussed on Belgian radio where the interest grew so much that the family story has become almost a legend in the village of Andrimont and the area; as we have learned from the many family visits made and from letters received.

I hope my book, in its simple and direct style of English, will act as an indictment of war, where the innocent are victims and where children have to sleep on bare floors far away from their cosy beds not knowing what tomorrow will bring, apart from more walking, fear and hunger.

The book itself is dedicated to the bravery of our parents. Maman especially, who was 46 years old at the time, whose calm and hopeful stance kept her young family together in 'no-man's-land'. And Papa who was 56 years old and did so much to allay the suffering of the young children and did not spare himself in any way.

Chapter One

10th May 1940 . . . .

The first explosion woke me, then came another which rattled the windows. I sat up in bed and looked at my sister Madeleine who shared the bed with me. She too was awake. Before I could speak I heard Therese, who slept in the next room with little Anne, cry in terror, "Oh Maman, thunder!" Poor Therese, every loud noise was thunder to her.

"Nonsense," said Maman, who had gone into their room, "it's a beautiful day."

This was true, sunshine was already streaming through the windows. "What is it Maman?" I asked as she came in.

Maman was looking out of the window. "I can't see anything," she answered.

There was another explosion. Maman crossed our bedroom to look out of the front window. I jumped out of bed to join her. Out of the window we could see, away across the fields, the yellow expanse of the Battice fortress. Planes were flying low above it, smoke was rising from the ground.

"Manoeuvres," said Maman. Shrugging her shoulders, she went downstairs.

I shouted to my sisters: "Come quickly to see, it's exciting."

They did not even stir. Little Anne was awake, and after quickly dressing her and myself, we went downstairs.

We joined Maman in the living-room. I had heard my young brothers running down the stairs before me, they were in the garden watching the manoeuvres. Suddenly there was a terrific roar in the sky. We ran into the garden. From behind the trees, flying low, came giant black planes, about twenty of them. We watched them pass overhead, we could see large black crosses on the wings. I looked at Maman.

"Come quickly inside, all of you," she said. "I think there's something wrong."

Subdued, we followed her inside. Maman switched on the radio. A man's voice was asking everyone to stand by, there was going to be a special announcement. Thus we heard the dreadful news.

War had been declared on Belgium, Holland and Luxembourg. The German invasion had begun at dawn. The voice went on but I wasn't listening any more. I was filled with panic. The planes we had watched, the explosions we had heard, were not manoeuvres, we were at war!

"Maman, I whispered, what are we going to do?"

Maman looked stunned. Therese and Madeleine, who had come downstairs now, looked frightened. Then we were all talking at once.

"Keep calm," said Maman. "Papa and Jean will have heard the news on their way to work and they will return soon."

We needed Maman's 'keep calm' for in our house the atmosphere was now chaotic with everyone, including the youngest, giving his or her opinion.

Maman was Belgian but Papa was British, and although we did not speak a word of English we were a British family. Our position was therefore a very bad one. Our parents had often discussed this fact since war had been declared between England and Germany. There had been talk of repatriation and of leaving our home in Belgium, but with a family of ten, most of them young children, money wasn't plentiful. The British Consulate had not been able to help. So there we were on the morning of the 10th May 1940, the war declared and us living, at most, fifteen miles from the German frontier.

All this was going through my mind, and with it a lot of the horror tales I had heard from the German invasion of 1914 which grown-ups were always ready to retell. I kept thinking . . . we shall all be shot: little Anne, Maman and the boys, it was horrible. Oh God . . . help us . . .

Papa came in soon afterwards. Then Jean came in. Maman looked relieved. We were together now, any decision to be taken could be discussed.

Papa and Maman were almost arguing. Papa did not want to

move. The British Army, he argued, would soon get to the frontier and the Germans would retreat. If we kept indoors and waited, all would be well. If the situation became too bad, we could wait in the cellar. Maman had no such faith in the British Army, our safest plan, she argued, was to try to get on the other side of the River Meuse.

Andrimont, our village, was in the range of fire from the fortresses which were our main belt of defence along the frontier. We must get behind them.

I tried to have my say but Maman set me busy helping the youngest ones dress in their Sunday clothes. "Just in case," said Maman. There was pandemonium again. Dressing in our Sunday clothing was exciting . . . it spoke of holiday and freedom from school. So we dressed ourselves and helped the little ones. I tried to listen to Papa and Maman, who still couldn't agree.

Maman went to the window, she called Papa over. I joined them and we watched a group of people coming down the road from the village.

It was the first of the families we were to see, loaded with all sorts of things and pushing a pram piled high with luggage. They passed silently.

"There, you see," said Maman, "others are thinking like me and leaving the village. I still think going on the other side of the River Meuse is the best idea."

Papa just would not see. He pointed out to Maman that, loaded as they were, the family would not get far, the children would tire and they would all have to return to their home.

I think what had given Papa a sense of security was the apparent calm now outside. It had grown fairly quiet; no more planes could be heard, only at regular intervals the firing from the fortresses in the distance. Furthermore, it was a beautiful sunny day and war seemed remote somehow. The morning wore on and I said to Madeleine, "Come on, we will go and see how the neighbours are doing."

We ran out of the house and out of the garden. We made for the cottages along the road near our house. Outside one of them our neighbour Mr Hislop was adjusting his bicycle. He looked up and saw us. He said, "Go inside to see Madame, she could do with some company."

Madame Hislop was lying in bed recovering from a recent

operation. We found her in tears.

"We are waiting for the ambulance," she said with tears rolling down her face. "I am going back to hospital. Monsieur Hislop, Roger and Juliette are going to try to go on the other side of the River Meuse, where Monsieur feels it will be much safer."

I looked at Madeleine. "That is just what Maman says," I remarked.

We had a little chat with Madame, trying to cheer her up. Monsieur Hislop came in and we watched as he made blanket packs, carefully rolling the blankets then tying them with string, leaving a loop to sling the pack across the shoulders. We were very impressed. I felt it would be a good idea if we too made some packs in case we took to the roads should Papa change his mind.

Quickly kissing Madame Hislop good-bye, we ran home. We told Therese about the blanket packs. We found some string and went upstairs out of Papa's view to make them. Madeleine fetched our new prized roller-skates, she slipped them inside one of the packs.

Looking out of the upstairs window we could see more groups of people going down the road to town. I felt we would soon be the only family left in the village – everyone else was running away.

Maman called us down to help her prepare lunch, it would have to be something quickly cooked. I helped to fry bacon and eggs while my sisters set the table and called the boys indoors. Jean was missing! To Maman's anxious enquiries, David answered that he had seen him cycle to the village. We ate in silence. The meal was nearly over when Jean burst into the room, fear and excitement on his face.

"Maman, Papa," he shouted. "The Germans are coming to the village. I have just seen some advance troops."

Maman slowly stood up, she seemed thunderstruck. "Oh God!" she cried. Papa also stood up and shouted:

"Quick everyone, get ready, we are leaving . . ."

Chapter Two

Eight years earlier . . .

Sometime, in my early life, I acquired the notion that my father was a fantastic person and that whatever anyone did he could do better. Possibly this was because he used to laugh so heartily at other's efforts to get anything done. Laugh! He used to roar and, laughing being infectious, we used to laugh with him. Papa, as he was known to us, had his own language which was a mixture of French, Walloon and English. To me, who could only speak French, this was wonderful. The fact that only our family could understand Papa did not matter. After all, it is very clever to make up a language. As we, who were used to the way Papa talked, understood him very well, we could translate what he said to anyone interested. Our young friends were given the impression that we spoke a foreign language, we gained their respect and we quite enjoyed being regarded as bi-lingual which we should really have been anyway.

Papa was born in England, joined the army in his early teens and had travelled the world with his regiment, the Royal Engineers. In 1914 his regiment was sent to Belgium. There he met and fell in love with a Belgian girl. He settled in Belgium with his bride and there they raised their family.

My parents loved children. Nearly every year a lady arrived with a suitcase to bring us, so I thought in my young days, a new baby. At the time this story starts, my parents had had eight visits. The score was three girls and five boys.

Neighbours were beginning to make remarks like: "How does your mother remember who's who?" Such a silly remark that was; after all, we all had names! I used to think that perhaps the neighbours were wishing that the 'Lady-with-the-suitcase' would call on them for a change.

One person was very unhappy at those frequent visits: our landlord Monsieur Denby was forever complaining. We rented his cottage in the village of Andrimont. He felt that our increasing family was stretching the living-in capabilities of the cottage to its limits.

I had never thought of it that way. Our bedrooms, no doubt, must have looked rather like hospital wards, with their many beds and cots. As I had never seen the inside of a hospital then, I accepted this as a normal way of life. Monsieur Denby did not.

One day he decided that he had had enough. As our tenancy contract ended the following year, he wanted our parents to find other accommodation.

We children were always sent to bed fairly early in the evening. When our bedtime ritual was over and we were all tucked up in bed, the girls and boys in their separate rooms, Maman would bid us all goodnight then, closing the door, go downstairs to what must have been bliss for her, with the peace and quiet that descended on the house at that time.

In the main bedroom floor, under our parent's bed, there was a kind of trap-door. It was a means of sending heat from the living-room to the bedroom above. Once Maman had gone downstairs we elder children used to get out of bed and, lying flat on our tummies, congregate around the open trap-door. Our range of vision was restricted, for the trap-door was squarely above the stove. Straining our ears we tried to follow the conversation between our parents. Some days all you would hear would be the rustle of newspapers. Maman would be reading the latest news, while Papa, who liked the sport of kings, would be trying to pick a likely winner.

Lately, however, with Monsieur Denby's unwillingness to renew our lease on the cottage, our parents were having long discussions on the subject of the future home for their large family. We sleepily followed these discussions. One thing our parents were fully in agreement about was that we would find it difficult to rent a house, so we must buy.

One evening, after another long discussion, Papa announced how he had decided to solve the housing problem. He would build a house.

"Where?" Maman asked simply.

There was a field on the other side of the land alongside our back garden. Papa would approach the owner of the field to ask if he would sell him a plot bordering the road.

To us, lying flat on our tummies under the bed, this was such great news that we had difficulty restraining ourselves from giving a cheer. Careful not to make a noise, we withdrew from under the bed. We stretched ourselves on our parent's bed and we started speculating about house building. We had not been consulted but we took it for granted that we would have a say in the design of our home to be. Jean wanted the house to be very high so he could fly his kite out of the window. Therese thought the house should be more of the style of the Palace of Versailles, of which we had seen a picture in a book given to us by our grandfather. Me, I was quite happy with a palace in the shape of a skyscraper. As for Madeleine, she nodded with approval at anything suggested.

Thanks to the creaking stairs we heard our parents coming to bed, so quickly we returned to our rooms and jumped back into our own beds. We were so excited that night that it was quite some time before we fell asleep.

Sous-le-Chateau is part of the village of Andrimont, to be found on the road meandering down the hill to the small town of Dison. It's a charming locality, where a few cottages and houses, a convent, where at the time we girls went to school, and a couple of farms are grouped around a 'chateau': a large mansion standing where an old castle had stood in earlier days, of which only the dungeon and a few castellated walls still remained. The chateau had an imposing arch-like entrance, in front of which was a small park. In front of the group of cottages, where ours was situated, was a large pond, railed for safety. Then all around were fields, a corner of one of which Papa was proposing to acquire.

When Papa returned from work the following day he dressed carefully. Then, satisfied with his appearance, he set out to pay a visit to the owner of the field who was also the owner of the chateau behind the park.

In a matter of a few weeks we were the owners of land large enough for a house and a garden. Papa immediately fenced what was now his property. Two poles and a piece of wire made a temporary gate. When we came home from school in the afternoon, we made a bee-line for our land, taking along the toddlers and the baby in the pram – Therese, who was the oldest one, being put in charge by Maman. We greatly enjoyed playing in 'our field'. To our young friends, who asked if they could join us, we shouted, "Papa doesn't allow it." The little ones simply shouted, "Go away." We did not yet have the manor, but we were lords and ladies already.

Meanwhile, at home, there were problems. A strike at work caused Papa to remain at home all day. There was no pay packet coming in at the end of the week. How long this situation would last, no one knew. With plenty of time on his hands, Papa started to dig the foundations for the house. After our school day was over we stood around the ever-increasing hole, a very interested audience.

There were other problems of which we were not, at the time, aware. The loan our parents had applied for wasn't forthcoming due to the strike.

Papa had been digging for a while when he found that the soil coming out of the ground was solid clay. His financial problems looming large in his mind, he must have felt like someone making a gold strike. Here was the stuff bricks were made of! He decided to make his own bricks.

Papa, who had been a Royal Engineer, lived up to his reputation, in my eyes, of being fantastic. He did wonders with a few pieces of iron. In no time he had made a brick-making machine; it made one brick at a time! So Papa set himself busy making bricks. Then he laid them out in neat rows on the ground for the sunny days of July to dry them. And so the hole became larger and the pile of bricks grew higher. Alas, the month of August brought rainstorms. The brick-making came to a halt, for there was no sun to rely on for drying the bricks.

One evening Papa was discussing with Maman his worries concerning the drying of the bricks. He felt that now he had no option, he would have to fire them. But this would make a lot of smoke and there was the possibility that the neighbours would not be very happy about it. He agreed with Maman that he must go to the Town Hall to seek advice and permission.

Papa, once again, spruced himself carefully and set off for the Town Hall. At the Town Hall Papa was taken seriously to the point of misunderstanding. A couple of weeks later, large placards appeared at strategic points in the village announcing that 'An application had been made for the opening of a brickworks, anyone having objections to this project, etc . . . '

Our parents were rightly worried, it being one thing to fire bricks for one's own use, another to start the proposed 'brickworks'. Fortunately people looked at our plot of land and at the existing pile of bricks, then went away shrugging their shoulders. No one saw anything to complain about, obviously, for after all the curiosity died down, Papa was advised that no one had objected.

Permission granted, Papa set about building a huge fire in the large hole. He had acquired some more pieces of iron. He made a griddle-like contraption and he laid his bricks on top of it. We were forbidden to go near the fire which burned fiercely. Of course, our neighbours were very interested. There was quite a crowd to watch the opening of the 'brickworks'.

Papa who, Maman told me, was regarded in those days as a rather eccentric Englishman, was giving the villagers value for money. Stripped to the waist, energetically alternating between the brick-making machine and the furnace, his concentration on the work at hand was totally unaffected by the fairly numerous sight-seers. It was early days, of course.

Soon the villagers realised the incinerating capabilities of the furnace. It was certainly a very handy way of getting rid of one's rubbish. To Papa, the supply of material to burn was very welcome indeed. So it arrived, in a satisfactory promenade of yet another old cupboard, another old chair; everything was thrown on the fire. Alas, one day, the supply of material to burn dried up.

Papa was a very ingenious person, but not a far-seeing one. When the last of what had seemed to be a never ending supply of fuel to burn dried up, having been devoured by the ravenous furnace, he arrived back at the cottage to seek Maman's advice. He needed her advice very much, for he had not envisaged a shortage of fuel. Maman suggested that perhaps we children might help.

And so, we who in the company of many of our friends had been an audience, became participants. We were sent to look around the fields for wood to burn. We were very eager at first. Jean was a very willing young boy, always anxious to pull his weight. Therese, rather a Madam, but still the oldest and always told by Maman that she must show a good example, did what she could. And that only left me, for Madeleine was a delicate little girl not fit for hard work, and the other children were too young. I was always eager not to be left out of anything, so with Jean and Therese we went in the fields all around us looking for wood. Of course, involving us was rather a measure of desperation, we found barely enough wood to justify lighting the fire.

The last days had arrived. Papa found it impossible to keep going. The 'brickworks' died a natural death, leaving a large blackened hole in 'our field'. But still the work had not been in vain. There was a good pile of bricks to mark all the effort. Three hundred in all!

Papa was still on strike and it was having an effect on his temper which was rather short these days. We all kept well out of his way. Maman saying, "Here's Papa," made us disappear. Jean and I were often quarrelling. We were close in age and I had a tendency to want to do exactly as he did. To Jean, boys were boys and girls were girls. It was as cut and dried as that. But now the need to keep out of Papa's way made us stick together. We avoided quarrelling so as not to make Papa angry, because when he was angry he had a voice like thunder and would shout so loud we were all frightened.

The house had to be built and September was here, the evenings were shorter. We children had lost almost all interest in the field. After all, what interest can a large blackened hole, a pile of bricks, and a now disused brick-making machine have for children who had dreamt of skyscrapers and palaces. Yes, we were disillusioned, disappointed and dismayed. We were now back at school after the summer holidays. The 'brickworks' episode had made us famous amongst our school friends, and our fame had dimmed with the collapse of the 'brickworks'. We felt it was time for Papa to come up with another good idea.

Our nightly vigil at the heat hole was still kept. It had not escaped Maman's attention, of course. Now and again we had the broom thrust into our faces, forcing us to beat a hasty retreat. On the whole, however, she tolerated it, for a while anyway. Then her voice would suddenly come up to us as a reminder that:

"I hope you are all in bed up there."

We would quickly leave our post and go to settle in our beds for the night. We had much respect for Maman whose word was law to us. She was a very good mother, very protective towards her large family and she was obviously tolerant of our childish ways. She understood that our little session at the heat hole was just a harmless pastime before we finally settled for the night and went to sleep.

One evening we heard Papa once again discussing brick making, the subject obviously still very much on his mind. We listened closely to hear what novel idea Papa would come up with. It was quite interesting. He talked about a water tank to be heated by – candles! The bricks would go on top of the tank. It sounded very intriguing, our childish imagination worked overtime, but we would have to wait to see the plans put into operation, we could not conjure in our minds what it really would be like. Of one thing we were certain, lack of money due to the continuing strike was making Papa very ingenious. We felt proud of Papa.

Some days later a large lorry drove up to the field and more pieces of iron were delivered. They did not pose any problems to Papa. Under our interested eyes all the pieces were put together to form a fair sized water tank. It was sunk into the blackened hole. With everything in order Papa started to dig another hole for clay. The brick machine was cleaned of rust and soon the brick making resumed.

The finished bricks lay neatly arranged on top of the water tank. Papa lit four candles underneath the tank. Maman had been dubious of this new method, as she told me later, to the point of wondering if Papa was perhaps suffering from delayed sunstroke. She kept a count of the number of candles used. Later on that night she told Papa the result of some calculations she had made. Papa could not dispute the mathematics presented to him; there was no doubt this method was too costly as well as ineffective. Maman had worked out that at the present rate of consumption it would cost more to buy the candles than it would to buy a new house. The new method was abandoned. More pieces of iron would lie in the field to rust!

Fate rescued Papa. The strike ended, he returned to work. Life returned to normal with a weekly income coming in. Soon we would be in a position to buy bricks. The ingenious brick-making machine and the water tank rusted in the autumn rain. 'Our field' now renamed the 'battlefield' looked in a very sorry state, with yellow mud everywhere and both holes filled with water. Any excursions we made to it were greeted by Maman on our return with cries of, "Take those shoes off immediately," or "Don't you dare come in with all that mud on your feet."

No one blamed Maman. The field meant mud, nothing but mud. And so ended an episode in the story of Papa's attempt to solve his family housing problem.

Chapter Three

Adjoining 'our field' was an old house, surrounded by its own garden, with tiny windows and one side wall completely covered in ivy. It nestled cosily against a background of orchard trees. To us children the house had a very intriguing look. Maman knew the occupants, two elderly persons, a brother and sister then in their late eighties.

The elderly lady knitted socks for us. Maman supplied her with wool and paid her in kind. The lady especially liked the jam Maman made. Sometimes I accompanied Maman on her visits to the old people. I loved the house, which was very old and, to me, full of mystery. Whenever I walked through its door I felt shivers along my spine. Surely if ghosts lived anywhere they must live here. Following Maman, I had walked through the front room and up the rickety staircase throwing glances over my shoulder, half hoping an apparition would materialise. Apart from the two old people, who lived snugly in the upstairs rooms, I had seen nothing. The atmosphere of the house had so fired my imagination that, once back in our cottage, my sister would listen with awe to my tales of the unseemly beings I had seen.

The old people's health had been failing for some time. One day they left the house to live in a nursing home. The house was for sale.

Papa, who had battled with the bricks problem for so long, cast an appreciative glance at the house. A large poster appeared on the house, announcing its sale by 'auction', whatever that meant to a little girl. The only auction I knew of at the time was the one Maman had won at the village fair one year. Was Papa hoping to win the house?

The evening talks between our parents speculated on the price the house might command. Our parents were really interested in the house as a possible home for their family. The plot of land first bought was alongside the house and it could easily be integrated into the garden of the house, so there would be nothing lost having acquired it. The house was old and dilapidated but it was large, there was plenty of room – and room was what we needed.

Knowing that there was a possibility of the house becoming our home, we too showed great interest. As well as the house there was the garden; we loved the garden. It was such an adventure garden, all paths, hedges and tiny gates leading from one part to the other. Made all the more attractive because many of our visits of exploration had been uninvited. There was a vegetable garden, a flower garden, an orchard and, to us children, two huge expanses of sloping lawn. Besides the fruit trees, there were also lilac trees and gooseberry bushes of very tasty fruit, as we had found on many of our illicit visits of exploration.

Oh yes! It would be lovely living there.

Andrimont was a village very like every village, in the fact that everyone knew and was interested in everyone else's business. Gossip was rife. An item, even of minor importance, in a village, becomes a subject for conversation until it has been talked over to the point of boredom. But an item like the sale of a house was very important. During the days that preceded the sale there were always interested parties lurking in the garden of the house, described on the poster as No. 6, Sous-le-Chateau. It was obvious by the interest the sale of the house attracted, although no doubt some of that interest was the result of curiosity, that if Papa went to the auction to make his bid, there would be other prospective buyers.

Papa was rather worried about the possibility of having to make too high a bid for the property. So as to deter would-be buyers, he decried the house to every onlooker he had the opportunity to talk to. Papa told them that the inside of the house was rotten and had only the value of firewood, that it all needed pulling to bits and dear oh dear . . . what a lot of work there was to make it habitable. Would-be buyers, no doubt, took a closer look at the house and in doing so they were forced to agree with Papa on that account. What they did not know and had no means of guessing, was that Papa had plans for the house. Papa, who had tried to solve his family's housing problem by first buying a piece of land to build a house, now had decided to acquire the shell of a house. This was how he regarded this house for sale. Should he succeed in his bid at the auction he would demolish all the inside of the house and rebuild it. Maman was the only one who knew of his plans at the time.

The auction was taking place during the week. On that day Papa did not go to work. What a morning he gave Maman! This was a very special day for him, a very special day indeed. It was a day when given a bit of luck he would become a house owner. Maman used to say that she had nine children, Papa being the ninth one. He was one of those 'Where's my' persons. Poor Maman, that fretful morning, had Papa to see to as well as the children who must be sent to school. Papa was unable to locate even the simplest thing like a pair of socks or a tie. Maman saw to his needs before she attended to us. So we saw Papa, wearing his best suit, his shoes a recommendation for army spit and polish, his brown curly hair neatly brushed – in fact, looking every inch the property owner that he was hoping to become – leave the house after a last 'Where's my'. This last one being his hat which he seldom wore but could not leave behind on this day of days.

Maman firmly closed the door behind him, but not before having given him a reminder not to go above a certain sum.

In our turn we left for school. Jean going up to the village where the boys' school was. And we three girls to the Convent, just a short way down the road from the cottage. The younger ones stayed at home with Maman.

For us at school the morning could not pass quickly enough. We ran home at lunch-time keen to be the first one to know how Papa had done at the auction. We were out of breath when we arrived home.

Papa was sitting on a chair, still wearing his best suit. Maman was at the stove cooking dinner. They took little notice of our arrival, but there was no need for us to ask the outcome of Papa's bid for the house. He sat there looking so pleased with himself that we had no doubts, Papa had already slipped into the role of a man of property. There he sat like a lord: Papa, the house owner, the owner of No. 6, Sous-le-Chateau.

Ours, I repeated to myself, the house is ours. I grabbed

Madeleine's hand, we ran into the garden and did a merry dance on the small green, singing, "We've got a house, we've got a house." We ran back indoors where Maman was smiling, she looked pleased.

"Did you win it?" I asked Papa.

I did not get an answer to my question. Jean arrived from the village school and was told the news.

"Did you give the most money, Papa?" he asked. Looking very wise, he added, "Pierre Malan's father was going to pay a lot of money for the house and he said you would only get it if you offered more. I told him you were English and the English were rich."

Maman said, "Sit down Jean and get your dinner, when you go back to school you can tell your friend that the rich Englishman, your Papa, has bought the house." She was laughing as she said this.

I knew Papa wasn't a rich Englishman. After all, he could not buy bricks and I felt sure that if he had been rich he would not have worked as hard as he had done in the 'field'. In my view rich people did not work, only the poor did.

"I think Papa won the house," I said to Jean.

Jean looked at me pityingly then said with scorn, "You are a stupid girl, nobody wins houses. They have to be bought."

I felt worried, what if Papa had spent all the money and we had no food.

"Have we got money left for food?" I asked Maman.

"Don't worry your little head, eat your dinner and be happy, the house is ours," was Maman's answer.

Oh well . . . I thought, if Maman is not worried there must be nothing to worry about. I heard Jean ask:

"Can we go to see the house?"

I joined in the chorus of voices that followed as we all asked together: "Yes, please can we go to see the house?"

"You can go in the garden," Maman told us, "the house is locked and we haven't got the key, Papa has to go and sign a lot of papers first then the key will be handed over."

We rushed out of the house and made our way to the garden of our new home. Entering it I felt like a queen, our garden at the cottage was tiny, but now we had a real garden. Maman had said as a parting shot, "Don't climb the trees."

We were all very good and did not climb the trees; there would be plenty of time for that once we lived there. We just looked around. I walked sedately with my sisters along the small paths. It was lovely to think this was ours for real. We had seen the inside of the house in the past and I had wished I lived in this mysterious looking house with its twisting staircase. At one time the house had two tenants, I felt then that the people living there were so lucky to always have friends so near to them.

Maman had friends from her childhood living in the village. There was Madame Fadier and Mariette, they called to see Maman fairly often and how interesting the conversation was when they came. Very often they spoke about the last war. They told and retold their adventures of the days of the occupation. Some of the things they had done seemed so daring to us, listening without missing a single word. This was perhaps how the people who had lived in this house, now ours, had felt.

The house would have to wait, for it was indeed locked when we tried the door. We peered through the small windows at the inside, it looked very empty and more mysterious than ever, we longed to roam through the rooms. Being unable to get into the house we turned our attention back to the garden.

The garden had obviously been neglected for a long time. It was overgrown, the hedges overhung, but to us this added to the charm of what was now our garden. The little paths in the flower garden were covered in weeds. In the flower-beds, fighting for pride of place with the marigolds and the geraniums, were buttercups and wild poppies. We loved them all, wild or cultivated, to us they were flowers. Madeleine and I cut a bunch for Maman, then we joined the boys playing on the lawns where the grass was so high one could hide in it. I could not remember a day in my life when I had felt so happy.

Maman came to tell us it was time to go back to school. What an afternoon we had at school. Therese and I were in the same class. Of course, the first thing we told Sister Marie, our teacher, was this wonderful news of having a new home. Sister Marie probably sensing our excitement, told one of us to tell the whole class about our news. I stood up and described the wonderful garden.

Julie, who was always a very sarcastic girl, put her hand up.

Sister Marie said, "Yes, Julie?"

"Sister," said Julie. "What Marguerite is talking about and describes as lovely flowers are nothing but a lot of weeds." Then she added, "In our garden Papa throws them away." She sat down feeling obviously pleased with herself.

I fought back the tears which I felt very near to shedding. I heard Sister Marie say, "Marguerite obviously loves every flower God makes and I think this is very nice."

I pondered this for a while, then resolved to bring Sister Marie a bunch of the lovely flowers from our garden. Never mind what that awful Julie said, buttercups were very nice.

Back at home that evening we were full of enthusiasm about our new house.

"When will we go to live there?" asked Jean.

It would be quite some time, Maman told us, the house was old and a lot of work was needed to make it fit for our family.

"I can help Papa," said Jean.

Jean wasn't very tall, but he had a lot of determination and he was quite handy too. I believed him – he would help.

Chapter Four

The legalities regarding the sale of the house were over. Finally Papa was handed the key. What a key! It would have done justice to St Peter, it was about six inches long and was so heavy no pockets could carry it, we always referred to it as St Peter's key.

Our parents went to look at the house while the eldest girls took charge of the young ones. We were all very excited, but when our parents came back and we heard Papa say, "The whole inside will have to be demolished." I said to Maman:

"We've got no house then?"

"Of course we have a house," said Maman, "but it needs modernising."

I was completely lost, Papa had said demolish, Maman said modernising, what did it all mean?

That night in bed with Madeleine, we discussed the matter. There was a new shop in town which had been 'modernised'. It now had a moving staircase . . . we felt that a moving staircase would be great. Then it had glass doors and marble floors. The more we talked about it the more attractive it became. Madeleine fell asleep so I turned over to dream of marble halls . . .

By Christmas I wasn't sure any more if we had a house at all. The garden, now covered in white with winter's snow, was littered with bits and pieces. At weekends Papa was very busy demolishing and by the look of the garden much of the house's inside was finding its way there. At the beginning Papa did not work alone, the village's gentlemen, or rather men of leisure, plus the ancient and venerable, used to make their way to the house. The village people, who were normally a quiet lot, could not ignore the banging and hammering which emanated from No. 6, Sous-le-Chateau. The weekends would see a procession of sightseers.

The weather was very cold, winter being very hard in the part of Belgium where we lived. The people looked on then went away shaking their heads, to be replaced by yet more people. Papa took no notice at the time, or didn't appear to. But when he returned home for a meal he would mimic his audience. One of his contentions was that the Belgians had one phrase to describe everything they looked at, this was, "Comme c'est beau," or "isn't that nice."

So Papa, throwing his hands into the air to add a bit of drama to the phrase, gave us version after version of "Comme c'est beau."

I had no idea what was nice about a house without an inside or about a pile of rubbish being thrown out into a lovely garden, turning it into a rubbish tip. However, it soon dawned on me that Papa was simply having a bit of leg-pulling about his audience.

Spring came back. The house had to be ready for September, when our lease at the cottage expired. Papa was feverishly demolishing. We had to keep our distance under strict orders from Maman, Papa must not be disturbed.

Finally, one day Maman told us that if we behaved ourselves we could go to see the house that day. With the better weather we had been spending more time in the back garden of the cottage. Together with the older children I spent much of my time draped on the garden gate surveying what would soon be our domain. We were longing for the day when we could do more than watch from afar. Today was the day – we were going to see the house.

After tea we all trooped over. The baby in the pram and the young ones by the hand. We were very excited, Papa had been so busy there must be much to see.

And so we first saw our house . . . I was shocked. There was the door, that huge green door with the large lock that fitted St Peter's key, it was open. What lay inside was, to me, unbelievable. There was the floor and the roof, nothing else! The wonderful mysterious house had gone, I turned away and started to cry . . .

I had known that the house was having the inside demolished, but to me that had been just a word. I had not envisaged what demolishing would do to the house I loved so much. Like a chorus we all said, "Oh."

Paul, pointing his little finger upward said simply, "The woof."

That summed up all, 'the roof', that was all we had; a roof over our heads.

The elder ones pressed Maman with questions.

"What is going to happen?"

"Did Papa do that?"

"Where will we put the beds and the table?"

"Where will we eat?"

"Come on," said Maman, "let's go back to the cottage."

When we were back home she sat us all down and carefully explained.

"Papa is going to build all the inside again and Monsieur Lebois is going to help him."

Monsieur Lebois was the village carpenter, we often saw him going past with his hand cart where all his tools lay. We saw a lot of him as the time went on.

One day that spring a large lorry came to deliver some long, heavy steel girders. Papa was doing everything Royal Engineer style as usual. The heavy girders lying in the garden of No. 6, Sous-le-Chateau attracted rather a lot of attention. "What is the Englishman doing now?" was the puzzled query of many who came to look at them. One of the curious onlookers was Monsieur Bollord, the village's constable.

Monsieur Bollord was a rather dour looking man who had the job of keeping the peace in the village. His peace-keeping did not involve anything really exciting like a post office snatch and grab raid, for there was no post office in the village. Or a bank raid, there was no bank in the village. I had heard how the greatest excitement in his career had been the day a pig due for slaughter had vanished overnight, and his mostly untried sleuth cunning had been needed to try to locate the missing pig. Ah! there had been a full inquiry into the matter, even a few anonymous letters were pushed in his door naming the culprit. The pig had never been found. But what a to-do for the village constable who had organised a legal search of all suspected farmers' stables. After it was all over it was decided the pig had been well and truly digested. The disgusted owner of the missing pig had made his protest of the non-return of his beast. He unloaded a heap of manure at the front door of the unfortunate constable, who had promptly arrested the culprit. On second thoughts, for manure was a valuable commodity, he had released him with a caution.

Of course, the fact that there was also no village gaol might have been of some influence.

And so Mr Bollord came to inspect Papa's steel girders. Papa, who had a lot of respect for authority, as an army trained disciple ought to have, then tried to explain the reason for the steel girders. Goodness knows why Monsieur Bollord was suspicious, unless he thought they were stolen property. Papa had shown him the bill, still to be paid, and had involved himself in a long and detailed explanation of why he was using steel girders. Jean and I had stood around very interested, after all Monsieur Bollord might well arrest Papa and we must stay around should he need help. Jean was good at tripping; that could be useful. Monsieur Bollord's face looked more and more puzzled. Papa was using his own language. After a while Monsieur Bollord had left, possibly not much wiser. However, he had done his job, being as officious as he knew how.

Jean and I were playing with a ball and as Monsieur Bollord's officious back retreated Jean threw the ball at him, he turned to find Jean asking innocently for his ball. Monsieur Bollord looked intently at Jean then he picked up the ball and threw it back. As he moved away we put our tongues out at him. Papa saw us. We both had a smack. As I said, Papa respected authority, local or otherwise.

The steel girders were put in position as rafters. Their place in the garden was taken by long wooden planks for the floor. The nights were longer now so Papa worked evenings as well as weekends.

We were still forbidden to go near the house. It was too dangerous Maman had said, so we went to school and kept our friends informed of any new developments we were aware of. We still kept our night vigil at the heat hole at bedtime. One of us who wasn't so keen to listen at the heat hole these days was Jean. He had had a nasty scare one evening when, having pushed his head too far into the hole, it stuck! What a commotion this had caused. There we were upstairs pulling at his legs, while downstairs Maman and Papa did their utmost to free him. We nearly had him apart. Jean was howling. Then finally he was freed. Naturally Maman had scolded him, he kept clear of the hole after this.

Spring had brought back the flowers and our new house had a hedge full of lilac trees. Maman loved all flowers but lilacs were her favourites, so bunch after bunch were brought to the cottage and our living-room was sweetly scented throughout the spring.

Summer was on its way when we saw the house for the second time, and like our first visit we went there as a group; a very eager and curious group. Maman had assured us that there was much to see. What a difference when we saw the house this time. It was really taking shape. There were four very large rooms and a nice curving staircase. We had forgotten about the skyscraper and the Palace of Versailles, the moving staircase and all our fantasies. This was much nicer, it was our very own home. Papa was building it. We knew that Maman had had much say in the design, for we had seen her, head down over drawings, deciding what went where.

"When will we move in the house?" I asked.

"In about three months," Maman replied, "when we have to leave the cottage."

Our summer holiday arrived. The garden of our new home had been tidied, there were no objections to us playing there. Soon after breakfast six of us, dragging our toys, would leave Maman with Paul and the baby Fernand who had now progressed from his cot to the playpen. We would run over to our new garden gate and let ourselves into the garden. The door of the house was locked, the garden was sufficient for us. Some of our friends came to join us, bringing their scooters and tricycles. What a lovely time we had.

One evening Papa returned from work looking very serious. He said something quietly to Maman, which made her exclaim, "Oh no!"

We found out the following day why Maman had exclaimed 'Oh no!' Papa did not leave for work as usual. Once again there was a strike on.

Breakfast over that day, Papa made his way to the house, and we were told to remain in the garden of the cottage. Papa was going to do some work where we could be in danger. We did not play that day. We stood at the cottage's gate. Loud knockings were coming from the house where Papa was obviously busy.

We were not the only ones attracted by the sounds. Monsieur Jamblon, who was so old that his white beard was nearly reaching his waist, ambled over. He went away and soon came back again carrying a pick. He went into the house. Then Monsieur Debrous, who lived in the village centre and was reputed never to have done a day's work in his life, something I could easily believe, for he always had his hands in his pockets; he too, went inside the house. Papa was later to refer to him as the 'gaffer'. Monsieur Debrous probably earned his nickname if he lived up to his reputation.

We children standing at the cottage gate were wondering what was going on inside the house. Suddenly there was a shower of stones followed by a big cloud of dust coming from the house. As fast as they could Jean and David ran up to Maman, who was busy inside the cottage, crying, "They are all knocking the house down."

Maman, carrying the baby, came out to see. Then, on seeing the pile of stones and the dust, said, "Oh good." She then explained to us that new window frames were going to be put in to replace the old ones. First, of course, the old windows had to be taken out. What we had just seen was the first window being demolished. All together four windows were demolished. When the work was completed, we were allowed to go and have a look around.

What a sad and sorry sight our house looked once again. There were gaping holes with ragged edges. Three on one side and one on the opposite side. With all the dust about, the trees in the orchard looked grey and the lawns were covered with stones. We were only young children and we could not imagine the difference that new windows would make. So there we were almost in tears looking at our prospective home. I was very vexed with Papa, for there he was, taking the house to bits again. I had heard Maman say to Papa that we had another three months before we must leave the cottage. How could we live in a house with large holes?

We could not keep a night vigil at the trap-door anymore. As it was summer the heat hole was closed and bolted from the living-room side. We were not up to date on the work taking place. Jean was allowed into the garden of the house. He was 'helping' so he was our eyes. We learned that one window was in place, then two. Then all the gaping holes disappeared as all four windows were replaced. The village carpenter had reappeared, with Monsieur Debrous the 'gaffer' in charge the work was progressing. Papa was still on strike.

The strike was obviously a very important one and expected to last because, though we were on our summer holidays, at the Convent dinners were being served to the children of strikers. There we met our friends once again. We kept them up to date on the progress of the work done at our house, giving a day to day account.

Julie was my tormentor, she was incessantly bragging about her mother's salon. I had asked Maman where our salon was, she had answered, "We don't have salons here, we have babies."

I knew babies did not impress Julie, who was an only daughter. I was really fed up with her salon. I took to telling her fantastic tales about our new furniture for our salon in the new house. The more she teased me the more inventions I made up. Alas one day she called my bluff so, hoping she would refuse, I offered to take her to see where we kept all that wonderful furniture. She did not refuse. Alongside our house, which had at some time been a farm, were some stables. They were to be renovated in the future to enlarge the house. For the present they were full of bags of cement, bricks, pieces of wood, tools and all the things needed by Papa for the work he was doing on the house. I took Julie to the stables. There was, of course, no furniture in sight.

"Where is it?" asked Julie, almost triumphant at having caught me out. I did my best to look crestfallen.

"Oh dear . . . they have been stolen," I retorted. I felt this was even more interesting, for now we had had burglars. Julie believed me, she went home and after that she left me alone.

That night there was quite a commotion. We were awakened by the Convent's bell. The Convent was very near us on the opposite side of the road. The ringing in the night was an alarm call; help was needed. I heard Papa running downstairs and out of the house. Maman came into our room to look out of the window. Therese and I jumped out of bed and joined her. Therese's teeth were shaking, making a funny noise.

"Is it ghosts Maman?" she said, almost in tears.

Maman made us go back to bed. "It's probably a little fire in the grass in the back garden," said Maman trying to calm Therese.

Jean had come to our room. "Can I go to help?" he asked. Oh Jean was brave! I thought.

I whispered to him, "It's ghosts."

Jean said no more about going out of the house, he settled for looking out of the window. The night outside was as black as ink. I sat on my bed beside Madeleine. She had not stirred. Maman saw me look at my sleeping sister.

"Don't wake her," she commanded. Maman had enough with three frightened children on her hands.

The bell had stopped ringing. Jean said, "There is no fire, so it must be ghosts."

I went and sat beside Maman and pushed my hand into hers, I felt very frightened. Therese also sat close. I thought of Papa outside in the dark night. What if the ghosts took him away? We sat for a long time awaiting Papa's return.

He came back to tell us the news that the nuns had had burglars; all was well now for nothing of value had been taken. The burglars were disturbed by the alarm bell. A number of villagers had come to help the nuns, but everyone had now returned home. As quiet fell again in our cottage, I snuggled back into bed. Then a thought struck me: Now nasty Julie would believe me; there *were* burglars around.

Chapter Five

That summer Papa was having very good weather and he was getting on really well with the rebuilding of the house. Every day at lunch-time he brought his two 'helpers' to the cottage for the midday meal. At night, when he returned to the cottage, he gave Maman very graphic descriptions of the goings on of the two men who were really more a hindrance than a help. Papa, who was very soft hearted, did not have the courage to tell the two men that fact.

Maman, who was keeping house on a very slender budget because of the strike, was rather fed up at having to give dinner every day to the two men who were nothing but a source of laughter for Papa as he told of their never-ending mishaps. Maman decided to visit her sister-in-law who lived in the village to explain her dilemma and ask for ideas on how she could deal with the situation. They put their two heads together. It would not be easy, for come midday the two men would arrive at the door of the cottage. Maman was a super cook. The men would not give up the delights of the lunch hour easily.

Maman came back from her sister-in-law with a plan of behaviour decided upon. She would undercook, she would overcook, she would give jam sandwiches, she would be late with the meal . . . But finally, Maman did nothing of the sort. That day, when the two men arrived, she gave them a piece of her mind. The cook in her had rebelled at the idea of sabotage and perhaps the loss of her culinary reputation, of which she was justly proud. She said what she thought and more. Grandfather Jamblon, his beard all a quiver, followed by Monsieur Debrous, his hands deeper in his pockets than usual, departed from our cottage and from our life, never to return. Leeches! Maman had called them.

They never forgot it. As for Papa, he was relieved, for really this was no time for laughing. He had a lot of work to do and only a short time to do it.

Uncle Paul was one of Maman's brothers. With his wife, Aunt Jose, they lived in the town of Verviers, about a half hour's walk downhill from Andrimont. He was a printer, having taken over our grandfather's business, and also had a stationery shop which Aunt Jose ran. Uncle Paul was a smart and dapper man. He was also, to me, a very mysterious person. During the 1914-18 war he was a member of the 'Deuxième Bureau' the French equivalent to 'MI5'. He moved in a silent cat-like manner, and always appeared to have a lot of secrets that he kept to himself.

Aunt Jose was a tall lady who always looked as if she had stepped out of a fashion magazine. She wore fashionable clothes and hats and always smelled of exquisite perfume. They had a great sorrow in their life when their only daughter had died at the age of six. At one time they had wanted to take Jean into their home and make him their heir. Jean, being his eldest son, Papa had understandably refused.

Our uncle and aunt were always very interested in our family. Very often they would walk up to Andrimont to visit us. Papa's house renovation especially interested them. Each time they came, the work done since their last visit would be inspected. Uncle Paul would go around following Papa, nodding his head with approval at all the innovations.

Our Aunt would kiss each one of us in turn on arrival and on leaving. I found this very enjoyable, she smelled so sweetly. Aunt Jose wore a small veil over her face at the time, as was the fashion. She would gently lift the veil before bending down. I found that gesture the epitome of elegance and always made a mental note that when I was grown up, I, too, would wear a veil and look as elegant as my aunt.

Years later, we learned that our aunt and uncle were both members of the Intelligence Service. They gave their life bravely for their country. They died in the horrendous concentration camps during the 1940-45 war.

To go back to the time of the story. One Sunday, Uncle Paul and Aunt Jose came to visit us, to see once again how things were getting on at our home. We had tea with them, enjoying the lovely gateau they had brought for us. Then it was time to go and make a little tour of our new home. We all walked over to the house. Paul, who was buggy mad, pulling his latest toy, David carrying the cat, Madeleine and I skipping on our new skipping ropes which Aunt Jose had given us, Therese pushing Fernand in the push-chair.

We entered the garden, then the house. The house had one room completely finished. Papa had even painted the walls. For the first time we went upstairs, two large rooms were ready for occupation. The new windows were all primed ready for painting. Papa had done very well. Leaving the grown-ups discussing all the house's new additions, we children made for the garden.

It was harvest time, the fruit trees had greengages ready to be picked. The gooseberry bushes were gorging with fruit, we counted thirty-six red-currant bushes. Quickly, we filled our dress pockets with fruit. We followed our elders home later and furtively made for the back garden, eating to our hearts' content.

I had heard Papa tell Uncle Paul that we would be moving in the house at the end of the month. I could not wait. Papa had been working on the house for almost a year now. Much had happened during the year. It had been very exciting for us children. We would not have missed all these experiences for anything, with the comings and goings and all the excitement they generated. But moving in; that would be the experience to top them all.

When our relatives left that day their last parting remark was that they would come over for the removal. We were starting school again early in September. I was really disappointed that I would have to go to school on this greatly awaited day, and so were my sisters and brothers. Jean said hopefully, "Perhaps we will have a holiday to help."

Of course, we did not have a holiday that day. We were sent to school as usual, much to our disapproval. When we came home from school that afternoon we had to go to our neighbour Madam Dinnis. She took care of us whenever Maman needed help and this was one of those days. We had tea with Madame Dinnis and we had supper with her. It was nearly time for bed and there was still no sign of our parents.

Madame Dinnis stood at her front door with us children around her, we were all glancing up the road. Then we saw Maman arrive, looking very worried, "Oh Madame Dinnis!" she exclaimed. "What a catastrophe!"

Oh dear, I thought, the house is on fire! Grabbing Madeleine's hand I made for the door to watch the arrival of the fire engine, Maman added:

"The upstairs rooms are unusable."

We stopped in our tracks to listen to Maman. Madame Dinnis had kindly guided Maman to a chair. Sitting, she explained how the plaster on the walls had come off in the upstairs rooms, and how most of the beds had to be put in the downstairs room. The disused stables adjoining the house had been arranged as living quarters. There had been so much to do, said Maman. The stables had to be emptied of all the building materials, then cleaned. Apart from those too young to understand what had happened, we stood there, a very interested audience. Our reaction was to find it all a very great adventure. Fancy! living in a stable . . .

It was rather like Maman suddenly announcing that we were going camping, we were always happy to do this, and now something very like it was happening. We were too young to appreciate the problems this caused for our poor Maman. We were now even more eager to go to our new home. Just wait until I tell my friends at school, I thought!

Jean and David spoke up, "Maman, we'll love living in a stable," they both said. Rene and Paul wanted to know if there would be horses and cows there with us. Maman stood up and gathered her brood. Thanking Madame Dinnis, we left and followed Maman up the road.

Very excited we entered our new home, not quite as we had intended, but by the stable door . . . The first sight that caught my eye was Papa, who was sitting on a chair looking very tired, our aunt and uncle having gone home. I looked around, the furniture was propped up at different angles as the floor of the stable was uneven. The light was poor, for the stable had only two tiny windows deep-set in the walls. There were beds along the walls. Maman's stove was placed beside one of the small windows with the stove-pipe sticking out of it. There were pots and pans stacked up in one corner. The table in the middle of the room lay sideways.

No . . . it wasn't a palace. Then I caught sight of Madeleine's face, she was in tears . . . and that started the flood. The younger children, not quite knowing what it was about, joined in, there was a chorus of "I want to go home."

Maman sighed, "Oh dear, just what I needed." She set out to comfort everyone by getting the biscuit box. She could not hand them out fast enough. I wasn't crying but I held my hand out just the same, soon everyone was munching and tears were forgotten.

Our parents settled us down for the night, some slept in the one good room, the others slept in the stable. Thus . . . we spent our first night in our house.

The strike was ended, but in the wool industry where Papa was employed the business was very slack. Papa returned to work on a three day week. This gave him four days to work on the house. He worked very hard to re-plaster the upstairs rooms. Meanwhile, we quite enjoyed living in our 'half way' house, although I don't suppose it was an easy time for Maman, who had to feed and keep clean eight young children in those difficult circumstances. Therese and I helped as much as possible but only in a small way.

The end of the year was rather mild weather-wise but, living in high Belgium, we had to be ready for what at times turned out to be almost arctic conditions in winter. With this in mind, Papa worked very hard to get the upstairs rooms ready for use. He worked to that end every possible minute.

A month after our moving into the house Papa had the rooms put right. As well as re-plastering the walls he had built partitions so we now had four bedrooms.

One day we said good-bye to our bohemian life in the stable. Not without a touch of regret because we children had found it fun. We came home from school one afternoon to find the house transformed. The living-room was now in the large downstairs room and our beds were distributed in the bedrooms upstairs. Everywhere looked neat and tidy. As the days passed we found it very nice to live once again in a normal fashion. We settled very well. We had almost forgotten the cottage and our landlord Monsieur Denby. He had done us a good turn by being so difficult about our occupation of the cottage. For there we were, settling into our own home with its lovely garden all around it.

We were very proud of the garden and many of our friends were shown around our 'grounds'. We felt as if we were taking them around a park with splendid 'flora and fauna'. The fauna being our numerous pets who distributed themselves about the garden.

The first winter spent in the house was very cold. At the start of November the snow started to fall and went on falling. The temperature plummeted to well below zero. Our gutters had icicles so long they almost reached the ground. Our garden was white covered with a thick snow blanket. Papa cleared a path from the door to the gate.

We loved the snow. Despite Maman repeating that it was much too cold to go out, we pleaded and pleaded until we were allowed to play in the snow. Maman wrapped us like mummies, even to putting scarves around our faces leaving only the eyes showing. With our wellies on we ran about in the snow making huge snowballs and snowmen. The pond in front of the cottage was frozen solid with the icy weather and we went sliding on it. Jean had a home-made sledge. He dragged us around the pond one after the other until he was tired. We had the time of our lives playing in the snow. Slides appeared on the road; these were made by the older children and we fearlessly took our turn on them. The scenery went flying past our eyes as the speed we generated on the glistening ice carried our bodies to a tumbling end. We picked ourselves up and started again. We only felt the cold when we were finally back indoors where we blew on our frozen fingers, not daring to cry for fear that we would not be allowed out the next day.

Jean and I had started going shopping in the village for Maman when we came home from school. Maman would check that we were well wrapped up, give us the shopping basket and the shopping list and off we would go. Therese was helping with the housework and Madeleine was often ill with sore throats. Jean and I would set off in the cold afternoon, Jean pushing his scooter which went everywhere with him. The roads were so bad that the scooter was only of use for carrying the loaded shopping basket on our return.

There were not many vehicles passing through the village; the bus passing three times a day, coal lorries, the lorries for the mill, plus an occasional car, made up all the traffic. The roads were not cleared of snow as quickly as they should have been and much ice soon formed on them. This made our shopping trips lots of fun, we took turns at sliding and pushing the scooter.

Sometimes when the roads were really impassable, gangs of men came to clear the snow. They would shovel the snow onto the sides of the roads, then when we went out we walked between what looked like mountains of snow. I really enjoyed this. Older children made igloos and passageways. We had such fun going around the snow roads and passages that despite Maman telling us to be as quick as we could when doing the shopping, we lingered. Instead of following the roads, the scooter with its loaded basket was laboriously pushed by Jean round and round in what seemed to be a never ending white road. Maman would scold us for having taken such a long time but she wasn't too hard on us. The snow had been a big attraction for Maman when she was young and she had been a good skater on these very same roads For Maman was born and had spent her youth in Andrimont, and she remembered the fun the snow had given her.

December was near, there were some anxious questions as to how would Santa Claus find us. They were simply answered by Maman who told us to join hands and sing. This was a custom in Belgium. Santa, children were told, was going around from house to house listening to find out if they were well behaved. If children sang Santa-songs and Santa was about, then sweets and fruit would fall into the room; a present from Santa who apparently liked songs. It was a custom much loved by children. When Maman had said, "Join hands and sing," we would form a circle and sing those little ditties, and soon Santa would prove that he was around as we were showered with goodies.

After a throwing session we might find our uncle and aunt calling in. They were just going past of course! The younger ones were taken in, the elder ones, well, they knew who Santa was. But as Maman had once said, "Those who don't believe in Santa get nothing." Unless actually told the truth by our parents, those who had doubts kept quiet.

Then would come the day of days, the day when Santa called to fill the plates. The custom being to put a large plate for each child on the table one Saturday night early in December. On Sunday morning the plates were found by the children to be full of sweets, fruit, chocolates and nuts. Then around the table there would be the toys for each child. Maman put our eight plates on the table with a large dish for her and Papa. To come downstairs on Santa's day was to us like walking into fairyland. Maman told me in later years that our grandparents and godparents had sent some of the toys which made this day such a great day for us.

Sometimes our English relations sent gifts at Christmas and

this would be an added bonus for us. Christmas always made me think that we had very rich relations in England. Our Belgian relations sent a goodwill card to the family but we awaited with impatience the arrival of the greetings from England. The postman would deliver very colourful and bulky letters and we would find in them cards for every one of us and such lovely cards too.

At the time we lived in Belgium, Christmas was mostly a holy feast, with the beautiful church services playing the most important part in that day. In our house the crib would be placed on top of the sideboard and we would say our evening prayers with the room lit by the light of the candle at the crib. What enchanting moments these were. We had a tiny statue of the Infant Jesus made of wax, He was very real to us as we prayed at the crib.

We had a Christmas tree made of holly where chocolates and tiny animals made of marzipan were hung to be eaten on Christmas Day. An added attraction was that this was one of the special days when Maman made her waffles. These were delicious and melted in the mouth.

All throughout that first winter nothing more was done to the house. I have no doubts that Papa was glad of a spell of rest for he had worked very hard during the summer. Now he hibernated, as Maman put it, just like our little tortoise Catherine. Hibernating for Papa meant sitting by the fire reading the sports papers to see which horse he should back.

Chapter Six

If there was such a thing as a 'Jack of all Sports' Papa must have ranked high for the title. He was interested in sports; all types of sports. He was always involved in some way with one sport or another. Maman, on the other hand, regarded sport as very good for young single men but very bad for a man with family commitments, especially if that man was Papa. Trying to keep a man interested in sport from indulging his fancy is like taking a bone from a dog.

When I was a very small girl Papa was a trainer for the football team of Verviers. Although I have no recollections of it I was involved in the team's training sessions. I went along with Papa. This was probably as a conciliatory measure for Maman as he could then say that he was minding the baby. Apparently I was taken around on the back of an Alsatian dog, of whom I was told I was very fond.

Papa was a successful trainer. This may sound very good to an outsider but alas it had unwelcomed effects on his home life. At the time Papa took over, the football team wasn't very outstanding. He soon changed all that in real military style. He soon had the team acting as one, all gunning for the same spot, the other team's goal. Up the league they went until the first division was reached. That ended Papa's career as a trainer, for Maman really put her foot down then.

It started slowly, when the flush of success was barely upon the cheeks of the players. The first win was toasted and rejoiced in. As the ladder of fame was climbed, the toasting and rejoicing lasted longer and longer. Maman, who was at home with her young children, awaiting the return of her husband, became more and more upset. When the game which put the team well and truly in the first division was won, Papa returned home full of jubilation; and drinks. We lived in town at the time, in a second storey apartment. Papa had to be assisted upstairs and once upstairs had to be put to bed.

The next day Maman issued her ultimatum. Papa gave up the football scene or she would return to her mother. Papa sulked for days. Maman won, he tendered his resignation and left the team.

For a while he passed his spare time taking Therese, Jean and I around all the monuments and parks of the town. However, it wasn't long before he had once again taken up his main interest, sport. This time he became a boxer's coach and masseur. The young man he had under his wing did not win too often. From Maman's point of view this was very satisfactory. Not having much to rejoice about, Papa came home more or less sober. By then we had moved to the village of Andrimont, and the boxer would appear regularly at our home. Papa, who was an experienced masseur, a skill acquired in his army days, would work on the boxer's body to make him fit. He did not make him fit enough, for the boxer did not become famous as Papa had predicted he would be one day. So the young man gave up boxing to become a milkman. Papa then turned his eyes to horses and we came to dread Saturday mornings.

On Saturday mornings Papa sat by the fire reading his sports newspapers to decide what horse he should back. He gave much time and thought to this task. We were expected to keep quiet; our chatter apparently upset his concentration. It was a difficult job for Maman, keeping eight healthy children quiet. If there was snow outside, even though it was very cold, Maman would wrap us well and we would play out. On wet days, alas, no going out for us. Papa seldom backed winners, because in the sport of kings the pauper has no chance. Of course, if we had been around when he made his choice, he would blame us for upsetting his concentration. Maman teased him about this, she reminded him that even when we had been out at the time he made his choice his horses either fell, went lame, unseated their jockeys or simply refused to move. Papa was, said Maman, the biggest jinx the jockeys had. Papa, furious at this would throw his papers on the floor and leave the room. Then, putting his jacket and coat on, go to the village to see Uncle George who had a large loft full of racing pigeons. One day, after a trip to the village, Papa came back with two young pigeons in a shoe-box.

Maman loved animals and birds, in our house we already had two cats, a tortoise, a little sparrow being nursed back to health and four rabbits belonging to the boys. When the pigeons were brought in they were immediately accepted in our household. Later on Papa decided to take up pigeon racing. I think he subscribed to the theory 'the more the merrier'. He already had eight children, a small menagerie of pets and now he proposed to add to his full household by breeding pigeons. Maman said nothing, as she had taken to the small birds at first sight.

And so Papa found himself a job for the winter. He built a loft in the attic. The confraternity of pigeon fanciers is a large one in Belgium and there is a closeness of ranks amongst its members. When the loft was ready he received gifts of pigeons. Soon he had six pigeons. Papa would go to the loft cooing and softly whistling to the birds.

Needless to say that we children were very interested. Our school friends were informed and Maman was presented with yet another of our young friends asking, "Can I go up to see the pigeons?"

Maman finally put her foot down here, going to the attic meant going through the bedrooms where the trap-door leading to it was. "You will see them in the spring, they will be flying then," she promised.

A lovely dark red pigeon had become very attached to Maman whose job it was to feed the birds in the mornings. We named it Bijou. In our constant quest for knowledge regarding anything new in our lives, we had learned that the 'Blue Riband' home flight of racing pigeons was the Barcelona flight. We saw in our geography book that Barcelona was very far away. To us Bijou, our star pigeon, would one day win that flight. He was very intelligent, he loved Maman and we had no doubts that if he was sent away he would hurry home. It's all so simple for children who have no knowledge of pedigree or hazards to pigeons on long flights. We did not know then that for our mother Bijou was a pet not a racing-pigeon.

In the winter the washing was hung to dry in the attic. Therese and I climbed up there with Maman to help, then we would stay for a while to watch the pigeons in the loft. We had given each new addition a name and Papa used those names. As we observed them growing we found each pigeon had a distinct personality. 'Cheri' or darling was actually very bad tempered, he ruled the loft and his rule was a rule of terror; his mate was called 'Joli', meaning pretty, and was indeed pretty in all its ways. Then we had 'Le Ramoneur', meaning the chimney-sweep, for he was always to be found near a chimney and once even found his way inside. Jean would sometimes join us on our sessions of observation beside the loft. He wasn't very interested. He had joined the Boy Scouts and had discovered reading as a form of pleasure rather than something one does at school. Children's Westerns completely absorbed him. When he wasn't away at a scout's meeting, he would be deeply engrossed in a story of the great Wild West.

Unfortunately the great Wild West gave Jean nightmares. Maman would be awakened by him doing a war dance at the foot of her bed and she would have to lead him back to his bed as he was sleep-walking. After one of his nightly performances he was forbidden to read those books at bedtime. Maman had more than one child to worry about so after a while Jean would once again spend an evening with his cowboys and indians, and as a result do a war dance in his sleep. We never understood why he would unerringly make for Maman's bed.

However, with the pigeons and Jean's war dances to liven up our lives, winter came to an end to make way for the spring.

With spring here, Papa turned his eyes towards the garden and . . . disaster! For Papa, who had in past years built bridges, had no eye for nature's type of beauty. He liked everything to be in straight lines. The garden as it was, full of little paths and hedges, did not fit into his ideas of efficiency. He had rebuilt the house, now he would rebuild the garden.

Maman did not agree with him this time, she liked the garden as it was and we were firmly on her side. She argued with Papa about the proposed changes. Papa got angry and when he was angry he shouted. Maman wasn't frightened of him at all. We were, of course, and the little ones cried, so to let the house revert to peace Maman looked the other way as Papa set out with his pick and his spade.

Soon he was pulling the hedges down. First between 'our field' with its two gaping holes and its rusty bits and pieces of iron, which previously remained hidden but were now exposed for all to see, to make the garden nice and square. This was regarded as a satisfactory shape by Papa. Well, it was square! . . . but nice? As I watched I had my doubts. When this was done he pulled down the hedges in our dream garden . . . one or the other of us would run indoors to Maman to announce what further desecration had taken place.

We children were dismayed, we had had such fun playing hide and seek around the hedges. Madeleine and I had pushed the doll's pram along the small paths, feeling like ladies in a park giving an airing to their babies. Soon there would be no adventure garden left.

"Oh Maman," we cried, "stop him, please stop him."

Maman consoled us: "We will have a lovely vegetable garden soon. You all love the nice soups I make don't you?" she asked, adding: "I need to grow vegetables for them."

I could see the garden with rows and rows of leeks and cabbages, and it was obvious watching my brother's and sister's faces that they did not envisage anything more exciting either.

Therese said, almost tearfully, "What about flowers? We need flowers for the village Fête." She was going to the Fête this year. It was the first time for her; the Fête was in July.

"Don't worry," said Maman, "there will be flowers for the Fête. The flower garden alongside the house will not be touched."

This was good news. I had visions of Maman bravely saving the flower garden, I did not know how but I knew that when Maman said 'don't worry' she meant it.

"What about the lilac trees?" asked Therese.

The lilac trees formed part of a hedge. Maman ran out of the house. If there was one thing Maman loved in the garden it was the lilac trees, lilac was her favourite flower. We ran, following her into the garden, as we neared we saw the remains of the lilac trees. Papa had cut them down. Tears silently rolled down Maman's face. Jean put out his chest and stretched himself to his full height. He picked up the lilac and gave it to Maman, then turning to Papa he said gravely, "You are a bad man."

Papa lost his temper. "Bloody flowers," he shouted. "The bloody flowers!"

We all ran away, we did not know what 'bloody' meant but we knew that when Papa used it he was really angry.

Indoors, Maman was arranging the lilac in vases and Therese

was helping her. "Go and tell the police," she suggested to Maman. Therese believed in the law. We had a cousin who was a policeman and everyone had to do as he said, perhaps he could stop Papa ravaging the garden!

Madeleine came running in. "Papa has made us a swing," she shouted.

We ran out into the garden. The swing hung from the trees. Soon we were all taking our turn on it and Papa could demolish the garden as much as he liked. We had a swing; we were happy.

Papa finished his work in the garden. Apart from the orchard where he had left a hedge to separate it from the house, the garden was denuded, almost savagely. Gone were the gates and the paths which we had so loved. In those days the garden was very much our world for Maman did not believe in inflicting her family on her friends. Only on rare occasions did we step outside into the big world, except of course for going to school. Despite the swing, which had brought some consolation, I felt that Papa was losing ground in my mind where he had for so long reigned as a fantastic person.

However, in the garden things began to look less bleak. First he tidied, then he dug the garden and presented Maman, who was the green fingered person in our family, with a large plot, rectangular in shape, where she could grow the vegetables she needed for cooking.

We helped Maman in the raking and sowing of seeds. We shuffled in procession behind her, firming the small paths she made between the seed beds. In each small bed a stick with a seed packet attached to it reminded what was planted there. Those of us who could read examined the packets, reading the names of the seeds, while those who could not yet read looked at the coloured pictures on the packets. We shouted to each other "cabbages", "carrots", "leeks", as if we were making wonderful discoveries.

It was obviously very good to have so many vegetables growing in the garden but Madeleine and I felt we would have liked flowers better.

One day, coming home from school, we met Monsieur Danber who lived in the last house across from the Convent where we went to school. Monsieur Danber was a gardener who grew for selling, he was also a bee-keeper selling honey. The bees frightened us because we had seen Jean getting stung. He had

Maman – Renee-Marie Keyeux, aged 26 in 1918.
Soon to marry Papa – David Docherty.

Jean, Marie-Therese, Marguerite and Madeleine.
In Verviers for the fair, 1932.

Andrimont.

The Docherty family, 1932. Taken beside the pond at
Sous-le-Chateau, Andrimont.
Back: Marguerite and Marie Therese.
Front: Paul, Madeleine, Danny, Rene and Jean.

The Chateau behind the park, facing our house.
Reproduced with thanks to Joseph Gelis, Foundation Adolphe Hardy
Dison, Belgium.

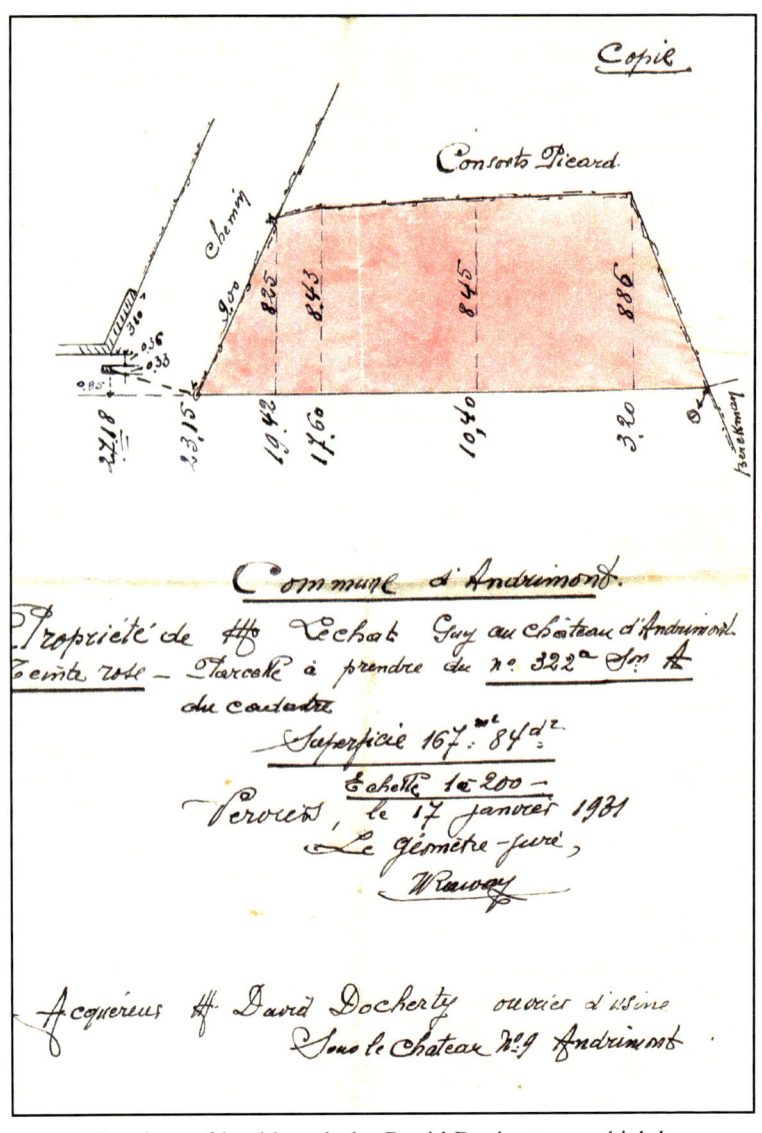

The piece of land bought by David Docherty on which he proposed to build a house. This later adjoined the house he completely renovated.

yelled so much that we guessed it had been a very unpleasant experience. Monsieur Danber, that day, was wheeling a barrow full of plants towards the pond, obviously to dispose of them. We caught up with him and after giving him our polite, "Bonjour Monsieur," we pointed to the barrow: "Do you have flower plants in there?" I asked hopefully.

"Yes," he said, "of course I have flower plants."

I knew this because he sold flowers for weddings and funerals. My question was really a way to start the conversation.

"What are all those?" I asked, pointing to the small green plants on the barrow.

Monsieur Danber, wanting to be kind to two little girls, said, "Do you like pansies?"

Did we like pansies indeed!

"Are those pansies?" I asked.

"Yes dear, they are pansies, have you not got pansies in your garden?"

I took him into my confidence. "Papa killed them all," I said as dramatically as I could.

Monsieur Danber stopped and laid his barrow on the ground. He took handfuls of the small plants then handed some to each of us. We received them with gratefulness, then we ran home and we went straight to the vegetable plot. Already cabbages were showing in their patch. We planted as many small plants as we could. Maman saw us from the window and she called us in for tea.

Indoors, we told Maman about the pansies. "Where have you planted them?" she enquired.

Madeleine spoke too quickly: "Amongst the cabbages," she told Maman.

I looked at Maman. She did not say anything. Later on that summer, whenever she brought a cabbage in, she also brought a little bunch of pansies to put in a vase on the window-sill. Papa did not notice the flowers. I don't think he really hated them, to him they did not exist.

Chapter Seven

Two happenings occupied us early in that first spring. Papa, when he dug the garden, lost the rhubarb. Then the pigeon-racing season started.

It might seem an unimportant thing to lose rhubarb plants. However, Maman made lovely rhubarb and apple compote which was a dish greatly appreciated when eaten with our tea-time sandwiches, so the loss of the rhubarb plants was not something one could overlook.

Papa insisted that he had seen nothing worthwhile keeping when he dug the garden. There were quite a few rhubarb plants in the garden, and as their roots were large it was hard to understand how Papa had not noticed them; he hadn't and that was that. So it was a question of waiting to see where the rhubarbs would finally turn up. We inspected the vegetable garden with Maman every morning. After many diligent searches, the rhubarb was eventually found growing amongst the carrots and had to remain there.

The rhubarb plants became a standing joke in our house as each successive spring they were lost at digging time, and it became an exciting hunt trying to spot them. Moved each year they survived and thrived at the expense of the vegetables in the plot where they were found.

The second happening that spring was to do with the pigeon racing. Chimay is a name I will always remember, it's the name of a town in Belgium. I must admit that I don't know exactly where it is situated. The pigeon-racing season had started. Cheri and Joli had teamed up as a pair and had produced two tiny eggs which they hatched in turn. It is the practice in pigeon-racing to race a pigeon that has a mate with eggs or young ones, for the urge of that pigeon to return to its loft is even greater. If I am wrong about this I will simply say that this was Papa's theory.

Cheri, the father-to-be, was therefore selected to be sent away for the first race of the year. The town to which Cheri was going to be dispatched was the town of Chimay. One Friday evening Papa went to town carrying Cheri in a basket. I have no doubts that by the numbers of good-byes he received Cheri knew that we would welcome him back, and as fast as possible if he were to win a prize. Later on in the evening Papa returned carrying a clock, it did not look like a clock as we knew clocks to be so we examined it from afar, having been forbidden to touch it. It was a very uninteresting square box, so eventually we gave up our examination and went to bed.

"Do you think Joli is crying for Cheri?" asked Madeleine when we were in bed.

I wasn't sure about this for I had never seen a pigeon cry. Not liking to admit my ignorance to my youngest sister I said that Joli would cry all night. Madeleine promptly burst into tears. Maman, passing through our bedroom, asked what was the matter.

"It's Joli," cried Madeleine.

"She is crying," I explained to Maman, "about Joli being lonely and crying all night for Cheri."

Maman said reassuringly, "I have just been to the loft and Joli is asleep, sitting on the eggs, so there's no need to worry about her."

Cheered up we fell asleep.

Sunday was the great day of Cheri's return from his first race. We went to Mass early. After I had done my morning jobs to help Maman, I joined Madeleine and the boys all sitting on the lawn awaiting Cheri's return. Therese, who felt that waiting for a pigeon was beneath her dignity, remained indoors with Maman. I could not understand Therese at times, she wanted so much to be grown up that I felt she was missing lots of fun. She even had a 'boyfriend' if one could call him that; all that had happened up to now was the exchange of Holy pictures.

And so we children sat scanning the sky, eyes shaded from the midday sun. Papa emerged from the house carrying a white flag; a handkerchief on a piece of stick. He went to position himself under the greengage trees where he had a commanding view of the loft. One of us laughed loudly, Papa's voice boomed, "What are you doing there?" He left his post and came over to where we sat, with a finger pointing towards the door. "All inside," he ordered, "you will frighten Cheri." From the tone of his voice we knew Papa meant it, so as fast as we could we ran indoors.

"Go upstairs and watch from the windows," advised Maman, who realised just how much we wanted to watch Cheri's return. She added, "Don't open the windows and don't make any noise."

From our vantage points at the upstairs windows we could see Papa under the greengage trees, his eyes scanning the sky for sight of his pigeon. We waited impatiently, one pushing the other to get a better look. Suddenly Papa became alive, waving his flag madly he ran about the garden. We looked for Cheri but there was nothing to be seen. Papa became more and more excited, he waved his flag with even greater vigour. We watched, mesmerised, for quite some time, then we saw Papa making for the door. We all ran downstairs.

We went into the living-room, Papa was sitting on a chair shaking his head, he kept repeating, "The blooming bird . . . the blooming bird . . . there on the blooming roof all the time."

Maman went up to the attic. After a short while she came down carrying the clock. "He's in," she said.

"Half an hour too blooming late," sighed Papa.

Jean said to Papa, "Can we have a dog instead of the blooming bird?"

Papa turned on Jean, "Don't you blooming well use that word."

We sat down to dinner at one o'clock. This was our first experience of pigeon-racing and I did not think I was going to like it. But like everything in life which is repeated time and time again, as the weeks went on and one pigeon after another was sent away to return to the 'blooming' loft, as we called it amongst ourselves, we learned to stay indoors quietly.

Then came one day which did not pass without leaving its mark.

On the Friday evening it was Bijou that Papa put into the basket to take to town. Maman was very attached to Bijou, she felt that he was still rather young to be sent away. She pleaded with Papa to wait a bit longer before racing him. We children witnessed his departure tearfully, even though Papa assured us that Bijou wasn't going very far and that we would see him back on Sunday. I think that Papa felt it was silly to be sentimental about racing pigeons.

Bijou went on his way. The following Sunday was very overcast. Uncle George, who had also sent pigeons away, came to tell Papa he had heard on the radio that unless there was an improvement in the weather the pigeons would not be released that day. As the day went on the weather worsened, by afternoon it was raining heavily.

We played indoors, and feeling somehow miserable we played 'Musical Funeral'. Some funerals at that time could be heard clearly as the funeral procession mounted the hill leading up to the village church and cemetery. When we heard a funeral coming up the hill we would line ourselves at the garden gate to watch what we called the 'Musical Funeral'. The horses would be dressed for the occasion in silver tasselled drapes and a very ornate headdress. The coach they were pulling was awe-inspiring, giving a real sense of the occasion. I always felt sad watching the cortège as it passed, I had heard that the dead closed their eyes forever until they got to heaven. I was sad that they would not see the light any more but it was really too complicated for a little girl, so with my brothers and sisters, once the cortège had passed, we played 'Musical Funeral'.

That day Maman had us going round and round marching in solemn pace, while Jean and David tapped a rhythm on a shoebox. Of course, that day we had Bijou in mind.

When we were tired of marching, we sat around questioning Maman.

"Will Bijou be home tomorrow?"

"What will happen to Bijou now?"

"How will he know that we are still waiting for him?"

Then simply a chorus of: "We want Bijou."

Uncle George, who had a radio, came over that evening to tell Papa that the forecast was for good weather the next day and that the pigeons would be released in the morning. Our long school holiday had started on the first of July. The morning saw us distributed around the garden awaiting the return of Bijou. Maman had said it would be near midday before we could expect to see him fly to the loft.

More than once there was a cry of 'there he is' as a large bird flew over. We went indoors for dinner. While we ate Maman kept a look-out for the pigeon, for his flight number on a ring carried around his foot had to be removed and put into the clock to record the time of his homecoming.

After we had our dinner, we all trooped out into the garden again. All except Therese who had no interest in pigeons, lost or not. We joined Maman, she looked really worried. "I wonder what could have happened," she murmured. Then shaking her head and sighing, added, "Our little Bijou is very late."

We all shook our heads and sighed. Even our toddler Fernand looked sad; muttering something totally incomprehensible, as he did not yet speak, he put up his arms to be lifted, I picked him up.

We waited all day for a sight of our dear little Bijou. And again the following day; in fact the whole week. Bijou never returned. I knew it was a real loss for Maman who just shook her head when we mentioned his name. All she said to Papa was, "You can look after your pigeons from now on, I am not going to that loft any more."

Papa was crestfallen and obviously very upset. He too could only shake his head about the loss of Bijou. "I thought he was old enough!"

There was never another pigeon loved as Bijou for Maman or for us. Pigeons came and went in the loft, some were lost, some exchanged, but no other was ever named Bijou. However, Maman fed them as she had done before, because she loved birds and animals. Some of the pigeons won races and Papa proudly brought home the prizes. Never once did we waste time dreaming of one of the pigeons winning the 'Barcelona' flight. Bijou's loss was felt too deeply. Poor little bird who was lost on his first flight after having been sent from the loft where he had been loved by us all. He was an omen of what the future held for us but we did not know it then.

Chapter Eight

Early in July that year I knew that we would soon be visited by the 'Lady-with-the-suitcase'. I wasn't fooled anymore for I knew now that the suitcase did not contain the baby. I had watched Maman, a normally slim person, put on a great deal of weight. I had heard comments made by my Aunts and by Maman's friends concerning her health. I had also watched, with great interest, our cat giving birth to kittens. I had made a momentous discovery, I had learned where babies came from. For confirmation I had looked under Maman's bed and found that the basket-cradle had nice freshly washed covers on and was full of things needed for a new baby.

I kept my discovery entirely to myself, I felt very wise with my new-found knowledge. We were on the long summer holiday. I was very much on the alert, keeping close to Maman. I was determined to be the first to see the new arrival. Personally, I wanted a sister, we had had four new brothers one after another. I loved them all but I felt it would be nice to have a little girl to play with. Madeleine had had a new pram on Santa's day; how lovely, I thought, to have a baby sister to put in the pram instead of the cat.

I kept my vigil and if I saw Maman sitting down a bit longer than usual, I would ask casually, "Are you feeling all right?"

Maman would look at me and ask, "Would you like something to do?"

She would give me a job like cleaning the lettuce or washing the dishes. Finding me following her about like a shadow, Maman probably thought that I was bored, she firmly believed that a girl was never too young to learn housework so she gave me small tasks. I would promptly do as I was asked and then once again return to her side.

My vigilance, alas, wasn't rewarded. The new baby was born in the middle of the night when I was asleep. Therese woke me up saying, "Can you hear a baby crying?" I was out of bed like a shot.

The 'Lady-with-the-suitcase' came into our room. "Sh . . ." she signalled, putting her finger across her mouth, then she whispered, "Be good girls and go back to sleep."

"Have we got a new baby?" I asked.

"I have brought you a little brother," she replied.

At that moment, brother or sister did not really matter. I asked to see the baby and so did Therese. After we promised to be good girls and be very quiet, the lady took us into Maman's room.

In the cradle beside Maman's bed was the loveliest baby that I had ever seen, all pink and white with blond hair. He was sound asleep, his tiny hands near his beautiful little face. I looked at him, lost in wonder, then Therese said softly to Maman, "What is his name?"

"Pierre," said Maman, "like Grand-père, do you like it?" she looked at us both.

We spoke together: "Yes, it's a lovely name."

The lady led us back to bed, she had said, "*I* have brought you a little brother," but I knew that *Maman* would now have bad legs, obviously having babies was bad for the legs.

Pierre was born the same week as the village Fête took place. We were too young so we had not before been involved with this occasion, but this year, as I have said, Therese, who had just entered her teens, was going and she was very excited about it. She was helping our music teacher run a stall. It was a day which Therese had looked forward to for a long time. Maman, who sewed all our clothes, was making her a new outfit; not a little girl's dress, but something befitting the young lady my sister was now becoming. Therese was very full of herself as she made her entry into her teens. This new dress Maman was making would, so she felt, put a stamp of sophistication on her. She had new shoes with a small heel to wear, now referring to my sandals as "your boats" which made me very vexed.

Baby Pierre arrived before Maman had quite finished the dress. On the Sunday of the Fête Maman sat up in bed finishing the dress. It wasn't long before Therese had her new dress on and, as Maman had also treated her to a hairdo, she set off for the Fête feeling very pleased with herself because of her new look and her new status.

Maman told Jean and I to keep the children playing safely in the garden; I was to help Papa making the tea later. It was a very hot day and the children wore the minimum amount of clothes. Paul had decided to wear even less than the others, for he had taken his cotton blouse off. Paul was still very fond of the buggy, in fact, if anyone wanted the buggy all that was needed was to look for Paul and the buggy would be behind him; he dragged it everywhere. We got involved in our games. A couple of times I went upstairs to see if Maman wanted a cool drink. The second time I went back into the garden to find that Paul and the buggy were missing. Jean and I looked everywhere we could think of for him, but neither Paul nor buggy could be found.

We stood around not knowing what to do, when suddenly the garden gate was pushed open. An indignant Therese, dragging her small brother, holding tight to his buggy, walked in. She went into the house and she marched him up the stairs to see Maman. I followed for I was to blame and would have to hear my punishment.

In Maman's bedroom, Therese stood, the tears rolling down her face.

"Maman," she cried, "look at this," she pushed Paul in front of Maman.

I waited with apprehension to see what would follow.

"He came to the Fête like that," she pointed at Paul who, after playing in the garden was black from head to foot. Therese added dramatically, "I was really ashamed."

Maman took the whole scene in, her young teenager in all her finery and the child black of face with cast off blouse. She said calmly, "It's only your little brother, it's not so terrible."

Therese, who obviously felt that the little world of sophistication she had built around herself had crumbled, declared, "I will not show my face outside again . . . I wouldn't dare." Then she saw me standing behind her. Furious, she turned on me, "It's all your fault, you . . . you . . . you'll never make a lady!"

I thought hard for a suitable retort. Maman spoke:

"Therese!" she said sternly, "go back to the Fête, no one will have noticed your brother and even if they had he is only a little child, you were a child once, remember?"

Therese went out of the room; I waited. Maman said, "When I give you a job I expect you to do it, you can leave me now, I am tired."

When I came downstairs Madeleine was waiting for me. "Did you get told off?" she queried.

I shrugged my shoulders and sighed. There was no doubt to me that having babies and teenagers caused problems. Then remembering Paul I ran out into the garden to look for him, he would not get away again. Meanwhile our new brother Pierre slept in the cradle blissfully unaware that he was now a member of the 'Tribe of David' as some of the older children in the village had nicknamed us.

Maman stayed in bed for ten days with our new brother in his cradle beside her. Therese and I took care of the house and family. Our Aunt Miou came every day from the village to help, and a very kind neighbour, Madame Jaquemin, came every morning to clean Maman's room and help with the linen.

Therese and I keeping house together was rather like having a cat and a dog in the same kennel. Therese, the new teenager, bossed me around with infuriating superiority. I was an independent little girl, I wanted to do things my own way, so life downstairs was anything but easy. Therese carried her grievances about me to Maman and would come back to announce to me that I was wanted upstairs, the look in her eyes telling me that I could expect a good telling off from Maman. Poor Maman, of course, was having a difficult time refereeing from her bed. When I appeared in front of her she would appeal to my better nature. Soon, however, she realised that only by giving each one specific tasks would anything like peace be achieved.

Downstairs, my sister and I practised the art of demarcation to its finest degree. We both sighed with relief when Maman came down once again and life returned to normal in our home.

Now that there was a baby once again in the house, Fernand somehow grew up overnight and really became one of us, in the garden he followed everyone as fast as his little legs carried him. Apart from the vegetable plot, the garden had been turned over to us, even the greengage trees which we climbed at will. To Papa, the greengage trees were 'the blooming trees'. He complained that they did not carry enough fruits to justify having them and that anyway the small crop they produced was eaten by the birds. Actually we ate the fruits but Papa was unaware of it.

When Papa had reduced most of the garden to an almost barren piece of land we had been desolate but children adapt and now we made the most of what was our playground. The lawns were still there and we had been given small plots of land. The boys cultivated theirs. The girls had grand ideas, there were many rock stones in the garden and we attempted to build a grotto to house a statue of the Virgin Mary. We were forced to abandon our work when the arched arc of the grotto was reached, this was something which we found impossible to make. The half-built grotto became a seat as well as a monument to childish endeavour. With Maman's help we built instead a house made of twigs and climbing plants where we sat out of the sun.

In September we returned to school; lessons and the Christmas concert rehearsals. We had had a wonderful holiday and we had a new baby to boast of. Life was very kind to us, so we felt.

Chapter Nine

In May that year I made my Solemn Communion. Each Catholic child at that time went through this ceremony at about eleven years of age. This occasion was regarded as a landmark in a child's life. The great day was awaited with anticipation, it was a real occasion in a child's life, both as a religious experience and as a day of rejoicing.

At home many preparations had to take place. A girl was dressed for that day like a miniature bride. There was the long white dress to be made, the veil, headdress, the white gloves and shoes to be bought. Then there were the day clothes for the following day which was a day of pilgrimage for the communicants. There was, of course, a lot of cost involved but aunts and uncles rallied around if help was needed.

Aunt Jose made all my clothes. Maman, leaving Madame Dinnis and Therese in charge of the family, took me to town for the fitting sessions. I was a very happy little girl, having so much fuss made about me and knowing that for once in my young life there would be one day which would really be mine, it was like being a princess for a day.

The long dress took shape and it was beautiful. There was a small frilled cape around the shoulders and a frill at the hem, the sleeves were long and gathered at the wrist. With the long dress went the veil and the headdress already once worn by Therese when she had herself been 'princess' for a day. She had been invited to the castle on that day to show her finery to the three little girls who lived there.

I had jet black hair and blue eyes like my mother. My Uncle Antoine, who lived in Gand had told me during a visit at holiday time that I was a very pretty girl. I had treasured those words and, in fact, I had taken to admiring myself in the mirror until Maman had reprimanded me for being vain. I still enjoyed watching my reflection but I always made sure before looking at myself in the mirror that Maman wasn't around. On the day of my Solemn Communion I would have been made to look as pretty as possible, so obviously there would be no objections to my enjoying it.

We had many aunts and uncles, for Maman had three sisters and five brothers. Apart from two of my uncles in religious life they were all married and had families. I received presents from each family, some of those presents were of jewellery.

Up to then the only jewellery I possessed was a small gold ring with a tiny ruby given to me for a 'Santa' day present. I also had a hat pin from my mother which I wore with pride on my beret. With the added trimming of a fox fur stole given to Maman by my aunt, I went to school one day in this grown-up attire! Therese, completely disgusted by what she considered to be my lack of good taste, had kept far away from me, even refusing to leave the house at the same time. Maman, probably amused by her daughter's adventure in the world of fashion, had left well alone.

Now I would have no need of cast-off jewellery and cast-off clothes, I was having my own finery just like a bride.

The day of my Solemn Communion dawned lovely and sunny. Three days previously I had attended a 'retraite' at the village church with the children who were to share this day with me. It was three days of religious preparation for the great day in my life. It was also a lovely opportunity to make new friends of the children from outlying areas who went to school nearer to their homes but to whom the church of St Laurent was the parish church.

Between the religious lessons and services we were able to discuss our clothes and all the plans for the rejoicing on the great day. Uncle Paul and Aunt Jose, who now had no family, had asked if they could give the celebration meal at their home in the evening. A taxi would be sent for Maman, the older children and myself, and Papa would look after the younger children at home. The thought of travelling in the taxi, wearing my lovely white clothes, was like a dream, for in my young days I had a great love of cars. I had much to tell my new friends in exchange for the telling of their arrangements.

The service of the Holy Mass preceding the Communion service started at 7.30 in the morning. We were up very early. With Maman's help I dressed in my lovely white clothes and was permitted a longer than usual look in the mirror to admire myself. Then, with Therese, Madeleine and Jean, I walked to the church. Cars with white ribbons went past us carrying other children and their families but we lived near so we walked.

The girls and boys making their Solemn Communion gathered at the presbytery then, following small girls dressed as angels, we all walked in procession to the church for the Solemn Mass. The church, beautifully decorated with flowers for the occasion, was full of parents and families of the communicants. Maman had the younger children to look after so was unable to attend, but even so I was happy that beautiful day.

After the Mass we returned home for breakfast, then with my sisters I went to see the neighbours to show them all my lovely clothes and presents. In the afternoon we returned to church for the Service of Consecration and Thanksgiving. It was a lovely and a very moving service with songs which the communicants sang with fervour. I felt very holy singing those beautiful hymns and my heart was full of love for Jesus and his Mother Mary. I had been chosen to read the speech of thanks to the parents at the end of the Service. Slowly, as I had been shown, I walked to the special place in the middle of the church and read the speech. It was a very moving moment as many mothers cried while listening to the special thanks coming from their children. After the speech and the Service ended we went back home to await the taxi.

At my aunt and uncle's home there were some cousins who had come to join in the celebrations. We ate a lovely meal, then later on we watched as fireworks were lit. Then finally the beautiful day ended as we returned home, travelling once again in a white ribboned taxi. It was a fitting end to the day which had given me so much happiness.

The following day, wearing more lovely new clothes, I joined all the children who had made their Solemn Communion with me, to go on a pilgrimage to the church in town then to a shrine in the country, where we prayed and sang with real feeling. On the way home the children exchanged small holy picture souvenirs of their Solemn Communion. Uncle Paul had printed mine. I was a very happy little girl that wonderful weekend, and afterwards I carried with me lovely memories of a time so full of beauty and holiness.

Once a year the children of the Convent went around the houses in the area collecting for the Missions. The children chosen to do the collecting were always children who had made their Solemn Communion. That year I was chosen and had to choose a companion. I wanted my sister Madeleine; she was too young, but the Nun in charge of the collection for the Mission must have decided that I would look after my sister properly, for she let me have my choice.

We set out one afternoon to do the collecting. It was a Thursday, the school's half day off. With a book to record amounts given and Mission leaflets, we called at doors on the route given to us. As a rule the villagers were generous, making small jokes about our quest for money, but giving nonetheless. We called at a number of houses, with the bag Maman had given us to carry the money being filled as we received contributions. Making our way through one side of the village we arrived at the shop of the coffin-maker. I dreaded going past his shop. It had open coffins on display. I knew how sad people were at funerals following loved ones lying in coffins, so I would shudder going past the coffin shop.

Monsieur Sanoir, the joiner/coffin-maker, was a man who liked a joke, despite his sad task. I was always surprised that he could actually laugh with the type of job he did; perhaps he liked money and did not care about people, was my conclusion. We had to call at his house. Madeleine's job was to ring the doorbells if they were within her reach. At the coffin-maker's she did just that and patiently we waited, gazing into the shop. Getting no answer the first time, Madeleine rang again. The door remained shut . . . then I saw a head peeping round a coffin; he is in and he is hiding from us, I thought. I told Madeleine my deductions.

"Oh that's terrible," she exclaimed and promptly she put her finger on the doorbell and kept it there. The ringing of the bell could be heard clearly from outside.

"We'll get told off," I remarked.

Madeleine let go of the bell but the ringing went on and on . . .

"Quick," I shouted, "let's run, it will not stop!"

We ran as fast as we could and as far as we could. Turning the corner of the road, we carried on our collecting.

About an hour later we were on our way back home. We had done very well and were very pleased with ourselves.

Reaching the corner of the road from the cemetery we went back into the village. Suddenly I pointed out to my sister the coffin-maker's shop. "Look," I said, "he's got the door off." The shop door was lying against the window. We trembled. What had we done? And what's more, we must pass by on the way home. Slowly and fearfully we made our way towards the village centre. The coffin-maker was very busy working on the door. We walked as quietly as possible until we came abreast of him. He kept his back to us. Almost creeping, we passed the shop then we ran for our lives.

"No use going back to ask him for money," remarked Madeleine, who now that the danger had passed was laughing.

Back home we told Maman about the bell and she too was laughing, then said, "Oh well, he should not be such a miser," adding, "but don't do that again, you are expected to collect from the willing only and leave others alone."

The next time we saw Monsieur Sanoir we gave him our "Bonjour Monsieur". He joked with us as usual. It did not occur to us that the removal of the door had nothing to do with us because at the time we did not know that one doesn't cure a non-stop ringing bell that way.

Maman permitted that we could go to the library after Mass on Sundays. Our village boasted two concert halls. One the 'Cercle la Concorde', a large building which had the library and the boy's classrooms above it. The other was simply called 'Chez Fabry', it was a hall above a bar and shop. There was quite a distinction between the two halls. Although most of the village population was Catholic, some practising, some lapsed, there was the Catholic School and the County School. Which school one went to decided which concert hall one attended; most of the time, anyway.

At the time of the story none of us had ever been to Chez Fabry apart from Papa who was a friend of Monsieur Fabry; a pigeon fancier like Papa. We had not been to the Cercle la Concorde either, we were too young for evening rejoicing. However, we were slowly taking a greater part in the village's life, and joining the library above the Cercle la Concorde was regarded by me as another step towards emancipation.

The library was run by one of the priests who supervised the outgoings and incomings of the books, plus the usage of the two billiard tables on the library's premises. Joining the library was regarded by me as very exciting, Maman was always very strict concerning what we read. Now I would be able to choose my own books; or so I thought.

Jean was already a member and when Madeleine and I walked into the library that Sunday he wasn't too pleased. I expect it was nice for him to get away for a while from 'the girls' as he called us.

Madeleine and I made a little tour of the library, having a good look around. Monsieur Polsen, the librarian, soon spotted his new clients and that for me was the end of my new-found freedom, for he decided what was suitable reading for me by sending us to the children's corner. And this is how I became an addict of 'Suzette's Library'. These were stories, mostly fictitious, concerning the capture and occupation of Belgium during the 1914-18 war. The stories were tales of childish bravery which both delighted and put fear in me. I became very aware, reading those books, that Belgium had had fearful enemies; the huns or the 'boches' as the books told. Of course, in the books children did wonderful things; they saved people from the 'boches'; they hid them, protected them, rescued them. It was wonderful what children had done; according to those books they had just about won the war.

I knew something about the war from my history book but I had never heard about the children's part in the war. I began to worry about a war starting again and about the 'boches' arresting and killing people. I did not feel as brave as the children in those books were. If there was another war I was ashamed to find that there would be no great deeds coming from me, no one would ever write wonderful stories about the wonderful things I had done. All I could think of, if another war came, was to get the family together and run away to England where, Papa told us, everything was wonderful.

Despite the fact that the books made me fearful, I read them with fascination. Every Sunday I made my way to the library for another couple of books. I read and re-read until I knew the stories almost by heart. When Mariette or Madame Fadier came to visit Maman I would ask about their war experiences, then Maman would talk about hers. The possibility of another war would be discussed. Thoughts were racing in my mind; fearful thoughts. I would have loved to dig a deep hole in the ground and build a house inside it to hide with my family and friends. Hide away from the 'boches' which frightened me so much.

At those times I was very afraid of the future.

Chapter Ten

We were in the third year of living in our house. Early that year Papa made a promise to Maman, he would once again work on the house and then asked, what would she like done first?

"The front room floor needs replacing," said Maman.

"And what else?" Papa wanted to know.

"I would love the house painted," was Maman's reply.

"Very well," said Papa, "I will do both jobs before the summer."

Maman was concerned about the front room floor which was in a state completely out of tone with the rest of the house. Because of this we children had a tendency to make a junk room out of it, leaving our odds and ends lying about there. Maman, up to then, had turned a blind eye, content that the rest of the house was in good order.

Aunt Miou, from the village, was having new flooring in her house in the style of the time, which was mosaic. Maman had set her heart on a mosaic floor for the front room.

Papa wasn't penny-pinching but he did not like to pay for something he could do himself, because one of Papa's contentions was that if there was a way of doing something, he could do it. One evening he went to the village to examine the new flooring at Aunt Miou's house and discuss with Uncle George the material used and the tools needed. He came home very pleased with himself. He assured Maman that she would have her mosaic floor and for a very low cost; just a few bags of cement. He would put a mosaic floor in the front room, there was really nothing to it.

"What about the small stones?" Maman questioned.

"I will buy the stones, naturally," was Papa's answer.

At that time Papa was once again on a three day week because of slackness of work due to international conditions; world-wide recession or something like it! Once I had asked Papa if England was the cause of all the trouble at his workplace. Because Papa had told us that at the wool factory where he was employed, all the wool came from English sheep, I wondered if the English had stopped sending wool to the factory.

Papa had been very cross with me, for there was I, only a small girl, and the daughter of an Englishman, saying something adverse about England . . . Yes, Papa had been very cross indeed and he had given me a lecture about how great and wonderful England was, how only good things came out of England. I was told how England ruled the world, how everyone was happy about this. Papa had concluded 'even the water's like champagne'. I had never tasted champagne but I had heard of it being a very expensive drink. And so I drew my own conclusions – England was a truly wonderful land and if there wasn't wool sent from England to be washed and cleaned at the factory of Verviers, this was because the sheep in England seldom needed washing! I wished that it would rain very hard where the sheep were so that there would be much mud to make the sheep very dirty. It had not happened and so Papa was on a three day week. However, there was something good about this for he had the time to make a mosaic floor and that would make Maman very happy.

Papa had said that he would make the mosaic floor but he had not said how long it would take him to do it. I heard him say one day we would have to wait. From my point of view this was far from pleasing, I had the job of keeping the existing floor clean. It wasn't an easy job, in fact I disliked it very much. I had heard someone remark about mosaic floors and on how easy they were to keep clean; all that was needed was to spit on them, so to speak. Having taken the message about those floors being easily cleaned, the quicker we had one the better it would be for me.

But alas, having decided to make the floor, Papa went one better, he set his sights on cutting the cost by using stones from the garden for the mosaic. To him it seemed idiotic to buy stones when our garden was full of them and they were there to be gathered.

One day Papa arrived back home from a shopping trip carrying a roll of wire-mesh. Oh! we told each other, Papa is up to something.

We gathered around to watch, first he made a wooden frame then he stretched the wire-mesh across it, the end product was a very large riddle. This done, he went to a corner of the garden and stood the riddle upright, balancing it on a strong piece of wood. When it was all set he started working, throwing shovelful after shovelful of soil onto the riddle. He soon had some help as the boys ran into the house and reappeared with spades, shovels and even tins. Everyone threw soil on the riddle. Soon the stones piled at Papa's feet – work on Maman's mosaic floor had started and 'started' was the key word.

The helpers soon became tired but Papa went on with his work. Day after day, then week after week, went by and still Papa riddled soil. He piled the stones against the walls of the house. It takes a lot of stones to make a floor. Papa was never daunted, he riddled far into the nights, and the clinking noise made by the stones as they dropped down the riddle became a very familiar sound to us as we lay in bed waiting for sleep on the then hot summer nights.

Then one day when there were stones all around the walls and huge piles of soil in the garden as fine as sand, Papa complained of pains in his back. We woke up one morning to the sounds of loud groans coming from Papa's room. Oh dear! was everyone's reaction, Papa must be very ill.

Maman came to our room; Therese and I were to give breakfast to the family and we were to see that the younger ones washed and dressed with as little noise as possible. I could see us all sadly following Papa's funeral very soon, so I did not argue with Therese at all that morning. If our poor Maman was to be a widow we must all be good children, I felt.

Jean was sent to the nearest telephone which was at the castle. Madame Ducat, the lady of the castle, telephoned the doctor and sent Mariette, her children's governess and Maman's friend, to help.

We were on our summer holidays once again, and we waited for the doctor while playing in the garden. In Papa's bedroom the window was wide open and Papa's groans could be heard. We were not carefree, there was a real crisis in our home. Maman ran up and down the stairs carrying towels heated on our ever-lighted stove up to Papa to try to ease the pain. Our family doctor arrived looking very cheerful; perhaps he would mend all Papa's broken bones I thought. Feeling pessimistic I followed him to the bottom of the stairs where I was soon joined by my brothers and sisters. We stood around waiting for the doctor's verdict.

Jean's verdict was clear: "He has broken his back with all the riddling he has been doing."

The conscience-stricken David was almost in tears. "We should have helped him more."

Fernand ran out, saying as he went, "I am going to kick the riddle."

I did not know what good he thought this would do but none of us stopped him; possibly we all felt it was a justified act considering what the riddle had done to Papa's back.

The doctor came down looking as cheerful as he had going up. He asked, "Which one is coming in the car with me to get Papa's medicine?"

There were shouts of "Me, me." A car drive was rather a longed-for experience.

Jean and I went with the doctor, and while we, feeling very grand, watched the scenery we knew so well go past us at speed as the car descended the hill to the town, Papa's pain was forgotten. Not for very long though, for soon the doctor stopped at the chemist. After getting the medicines we returned home, climbing the hill in the heat of the afternoon. Maman had cool drinks waiting for us when we arrived home then she disappeared upstairs with the medicines to minister to the ailing member of our family.

Papa stayed in bed for two weeks. He was suffering from strained ligaments and rheumatism. Finally he came downstairs looking the shadow of his former self. With Maman's help he made a circular tent with an open top, it was erected in the back garden where he sunbathed in the all-together to speed his recovery. We were forbidden to go near the tent for modesty's sake. Alas the sunshine cure did nothing for Papa's recovery. He fell asleep in the nude in the hot afternoon sun and soon he was back in bed with another complaint – severe sunburn!

Once again his cries of pain echoed in our home, much to the concern of us all. As Maman said later when Papa was fully recovered, she did not know what had been worse, the illness or the sunshine cure!

When Papa felt quite recovered he resumed his work. Soon he decided that there were enough stones for the floor. Stage two had been reached, the stones had to be washed. Papa found water at the pond across the road from the cottages. Backwards and forwards he went on his water trek. He washed the stones in an old bath tub. I had seen my Aunt's floor, the mosaic was made of multi-coloured stones; the washed stones would be ideal, I felt, and soon we would have a lovely floor, Papa was indeed clever!

The washing of the stones took quite a time because there were so many piles, but the day came when it was all done, I don't think Papa liked that phase of the floor making much for the stones had become the 'damn blooming stones' and as he worked great sighs were heard. The biggest sigh came when the last stones, cleaned and colourful, emerged from the bath tub; it was, of course, a sigh of relief which was echoed by all, most of all by me who could not wait to see the floor done.

Stage three – the making of the floor had arrived. With a small army of children running to and fro through the front room on their way in and out of the garden this had to be planned like a military operation; not a difficult thing for Papa with his army training. As he worked laying the stones and encasing them in cement, we found the pattern of wooden planks we had to walk on to get in or out, changing from day to day. When one of us was unfortunate to over-balance and a footstep appeared on the newly laid floor, heaven help the owner of the shoe who fitted the tell-tale imprint – we had not heard of the inquisition but we knew how it felt.

Finally the day came when the floor was laid and dry. Stage four had been reached – the sanding of the floor. Papa tried every method he could think of to make this part of the work easier. First he went down on his knees with a large pumice stone in his hands; he rubbed and rubbed but his progress was so slow that it seemed it would take a lifetime to do the floor. He tied sandpaper around a large broom; the best of that method was that he could stand to do the rubbing, the worst was that the results were nil. Then he made a heavy contraption, looking like the electric sander used by the people who made mosaic floors, and underneath this contraption he encased a number of pumice stones. Dragging the heavy 'sander' back and forth Papa did the work of ten men and he was rewarded when powdered grey dust appeared on the floor and the stones took on a glazed effect. It took a long time to do the whole floor. Maman suggested more than once to get the floor makers to finish the work. Papa would not accept defeat.

One never-to-be-forgotten day I was able to clean the floor – not with a spit – it did not have quite that quality. Nevertheless it looked nice. None of us doubted that the Royal engineers would have been proud of Papa.

Chapter Eleven

The feast of Corpus Christy is a great feast day on the Catholic calendar. It was celebrated throughout the country. On that day the Grande Procession took place in our village. As most of the villagers were Catholics the procession was regarded as a main ceremony in the religious life of the village. It was also a very great day for the school children who staged most of the tableaus and scenes from the Bible depicted in the procession.

A couple of weeks before, at the Convent, there were rehearsals where we children were shown how to walk with decorum in tune to marching music. Mère Supérieure assembled the girls in the school yard a few days before the feast. Reading from a list she held in her hand she would assign to each girl the part she would play in the procession. There were, of course, favourite parts and not so favourite parts. The tableaus and scenes being the same each year, we knew beforehand what the list consisted of, the concern was where in the list did our name fall?

Because the procession lasted about two and a half hours, we children carried something to sustain us on this long walk. Sweets were the general choice, considered to possess revitalising properties; children will be children! If your part in the procession decreed that you carried a vessel of some kind, such as a bowl of grapes, a basket of wheat or such, then the sweets you carried presented no problems. If, on the other hand, you were a crusader or formed part of a rosary with simply a paper rose attached to your shoulder, you were forced to carry your sustenance in your hand, and the Sweets would get very sticky in the almost inevitably hot weather at that time of year which was the end of June.

We all loved the Grande Procession. It was a real feast day for our village. The church was beautifully decorated and the holy statues to be carried in the procession were cleaned and dusted for their yearly outing. Houses along the route followed were flying the flag, and windows were decorated with best lace cloths, holy pictures and flowers in profusion. The roads along which the procession passed were strewn with flowers.

In our house Maman, who had five children taking part in the procession, had been very busy getting our clothes ready. The girls would leave the house dressed in white, the boys dressed in sailor suits.

Earlier that year Papa had promised to paint the house, but he had his task cut out doing the mosaic floor. However, he meant to keep his promise and had told Maman that she could count on the house being white for the day of the Grande Procession.

Papa, as usual, planned this task to its basic principle. Where other people doing the same job bought the necessary lime ready to use, Papa had bought the lime stones, then using an old barrel and water from the pond he slaked the stones to make his own lime. A lot of 'bloodys' were heard if we went near. We quickly took the message and watched from afar. The lime was poured into a home-made lime pit and as this was very dangerous for children the pit was covered with wooden planks. The lime had been there for a couple of months with Papa working hard on the mosaic floor, as well as racing pigeons . . .

Maman had given up the idea of a white house for the day promised. So when, the evening before the procession, Papa took out his ladder, his pail and his brush, Maman said, "What are you doing?"

"You can all go to bed," assured Papa. "When you get up tomorrow the house will be white."

In bed Madeleine and I agreed that it would be lovely to have a white house awaiting us in the morning, the morning of a very special day.

We awoke the morning of the Procession aware immediately of the day's occasion. Then we remembered the house, now apparently beautifully white. Maman was getting up, we joined her and ran with her into the garden to see the house. The sight which met our eyes was incredible. I felt I was dreaming . . .

The house was as it had been . . . there was not a trace of white on it. We could not believe our eyes. Maman kept saying, "He worked all night! What happened?"

We went indoors very disappointed, but it was the day of the Grande Procession and soon our family was getting itself ready for this greatly awaited day. When Therese, Madeleine and I were dressed in our white dresses we set out for the Convent where all the girls assembled to be fitted with the clothes for the part they took in the procession. I was a crusader, I wore a tunic edged with gold trimmings and a headband with a cross at the front. Madeleine had a large paper rose attached to her shoulder, she would hold on to a coloured cord forming a rosary, to mark the place as a rosary bead. Therese, dressed in a long flowing white dress with large wings across her shoulders, was the angel Gabriel.

We all went to Mass, then after Mass the procession was formed with everyone taking his or her allotted place. The band heading the procession started playing, and marching in step to its resounding tunes the procession made its way around the village, then the surrounding areas, calling at farms where home-made altars had been built. It was a wonderful display of religious fervour, full of beauty and blessings.

Our village priests, dressed in white and gold vestments, took turns in carrying the Monstrance under a dais of purple and gold carried by parishioners. Short services of Benediction were given at the altars built along the route.

Slowly the Grande Procession wound its way through the countryside around Andrimont. We walked for what appeared to be many kilometres. We sang and we prayed.

And because children are children, holy or otherwise, we munched our sweets until some of us were sick, we drank too much of the refreshing drinks provided by farmers with dire results – frequent visits to hedges. And as the time went on we dragged our feet more and more. But when finally the procession, on its way back to the starting place, arrived at the Convent, we were all revived. At the Convent the nuns had the most beautiful altar we had yet seen. Each successive year Mère Supérieure, who designed the decorations, surpassed herself; the halt there was always longer. Many mothers brought young children to join the procession for the final return to church.

On our way to the village we passed our home. Maman had decorated all the windows, the Belgian flag flew from the roof.

We got a wave from the rest of the family assembled in front of the house to watch the passing of the Grande Procession. Back in the village a huge altar had been built and for the last time that day benediction was given while fireworks detonated to let the surrounding areas participate in this final act. It had been a wonderful experience. We returned home tired but sorry that this occasion was finished until the following year.

We were ready for our dinner when we reached home and we had plenty of experiences to tell Maman. When we had gone over all the incidents that made this day so special, I remembered the house and Papa's work during the night, and his assurance that the house would be white by morning.

"What happened to the house Maman, did he not do it?"

"Oh yes," said Maman, "he did it all right."

"Then why is the house not white?" asked Therese.

"For a very simple reason," was Maman's answer. "You see, your father forgot to put the lime in the pails of water. What he really did was wash the house!"

There's no doubt, I thought, Papa really has strange ways.

Maman added, "You should have seen his face when he came down and went to look at his work."

Jean said, shaking his head, "Houly, houly, houly."

"Exactly," said Maman, "he said it a dozen times."

Houly . . . houly . . . houly . . . was always the way Papa reacted when he was flabbergasted. We never learned what 'houly' stood for but we heard it often.

Chapter Twelve

Up to now I have only spoken of how Papa's army training affected the ups and downs of his life as head of a large family. It also affected our personal life, for he expected us to copy him.

Papa always maintained a military bearing. He walked placing his feet in precise fashion, his arms swinging in rhythm at his sides, his shoulders thrown well back, his head high. Although he was of modest stature his bearing commended attention.

Having a father who had a military style was all very well but the day we grew out of the nappies stage and stood up on our tiny legs we found ourselves being trained to adopt the same stance, and when Papa started training us to walk in this marching fashion, we regarded it as a form of punishment. Nevertheless, when Papa was around we would almost automatically throw our shoulders back and straighten our spines. We soon learned to anticipate his "Stand straight!" or "Shoulders back!" As for the boys, he would admonish them, ordering, "Take your hands out of your pockets," and "Don't slouch."

As the years passed we were more and more the object of Papa's attention regarding our bearing and, of course, we hated it. As soon as he was out of sight down came our shoulders and we would revert to being children rather than miniature military machines.

Maman said very little about this; well she had married Papa so I presume she liked the way he walked. I liked it myself; for one thing we could spot Papa miles away, which was good if we were doing something he regarded as not done by girls. This was another of Papa's bugbears – girls must behave like girls and boys like boys, there was no room for a tomboy in our family or vice-versa.

One thing which he particularly disliked was Maman's giving in to the fashion of the time, allowing boys who had lovely curly hair to wear it shoulder length. Maman was like every young mother; proud of the beauty in her children. Two of my brothers wore their hair shoulder length style. Paul, who had lovely black ringlets and David, whose curly hair was a mother's pride. She ignored Papa dubbing the boys 'sissies' until the boys were of school age when the scissors were applied. When Paul lost his beautiful locks I was old enough to be dismayed at finding my little brother, whose hair had cascaded so gracefully around his neck, turned overnight into an almost hairless boy. I had been so happy taking him around and hearing grown-ups comment on his lovely hair. For some time I had kept a ringlet in an envelope as a souvenir. One day, like most things in the life of a child, it had disappeared. It was probably disposed of as rubbish by Maman who could not afford to let our possessions accumulate for fear the house would be full of them.

We used to collect like magpies. In the summer we had boxes and tins full of flying beetles, small lizards, tiny frogs, ladybirds, butterflies and dragon flies. No wonder Maman had clearance days! Life would have been impossible without those days.

I always knew when one of those 'clear-the-deck' days had taken place, for there would be our home, looking like a new pin, not a thing out of place. We would sit around looking at each other, not daring to upset anything. Maman would give us a lecture concerning our untidy habits, our proposed reformation and what she intended for the future. We listened, Madeleine would giggle, Maman had a soft spot for her as she was so delicate, a puff of wind would blow her away as Maman said, so she giggled and nothing was said. Jean would look very seriously at our parent during the lecture, probably wondering what he would do with whatever he was thinking of collecting next. Therese was fully on Maman's side, she being the eldest had to help in the cleaning sessions. David, who was the biggest magpie of us all and possessed an ancient handbag of large capacity into which went everything he could lay his hands on, including the best spoons, the thimble and the nail scissors, would be standing around lost in dreams, taking absolutely no notice. The same thing applied to the younger members of our family. As for me I was philosophical, I knew that Maman was greatly interested in nature and all its wonders. The next interesting butterfly we brought in would be examined just as closely by her as by ourselves, in fact she would help us store it without damage. But I knew that Mamans must also act as Mamans and this was only one of her 'I am the head' days; all Mamans had them. Possibly guessing my thoughts she would turn to me saying, "I mean you as well."

Then to change the subject I would say something like: "Do you want any messages?" or "Will I peel the potatoes?"

Maman, satisfied that she had got her message through to her brood, would let the house return to normal. As for me, very likely, as I was so willing, I would be given some task.

To us Maman was almost fearless. In a large family it only takes one child to imagine something for it to be declared a fact by the rest of the brood. Thus, if one of us declared that he or she has heard something moving in the garden in the dark of the evening, there would be a chorus of "That's right, I heard it too." Generally Maman ignored these declarations of impending danger, but if we seemed too upset by whatever invention our ever-active imaginations had conjured, then she would say, "I will go to have a look, stay where you are."

Children are such that in even the most feared situation, if an adult they trust explores, they will be close behind so as not to miss anything – be it ghost, devil, witch or whatever in a child's mind dwells outside at night time.

Maman never showed any signs of fear and she would simply go outside and have a good look around, with us in her wake. The dark shadows of the night would recede as she announced, "There is nothing there at all," and so no reasons at all to be afraid.

There was one thing, however, which upset Maman – she hated thunderstorms. In Andrimont, perched on top of a hill in high Belgium, surrounded by the wooded region of the Fagnes, thunderstorms were a certainty and very severe they were too.

We could always tell when a storm was in the air, the trees were still with not even the slightest trace of a breeze, the atmosphere was heavy, almost brooding. The only birds to be seen were the swallows flying low over the pond, all the other birds having vanished out of sight, leaving us without the sounds of their songs.

In our house Maman would start on a routine never varied. She would go around the house securing windows, closing internal doors and putting away into drawers everything made of steel. As the storm's first rumblings were heard she would gather us around her and burn some blessed box-tree cuttings while we said a prayer. This done we would await the fury of the storm, Maman feeling that she had done everything in her power to keep her family safe.

There were times when a storm would rage and some of us were away from home. Maman would be really upset at those times and very worried. Maman had a very good reason for her fear of thunderstorms, her friend aged eighteen had been struck dead by lightning while they were both returning home. Although this was some years past Maman had never forgotten the terrible experience. Now she firmly believed in being indoors during a storm, and staying away from windows and the stove. With all this to keep in mind thunderstorms were a major crisis in our life. We all feared them, Therese to the point of hiding inside a wardrobe or any handy cupboard.

One night there was a particularly vicious storm accompanied by gale force winds and an upstairs window was blown open with such a force that it sent a heavy brass ornament clattering down the stairs. The gust of wind then lifted the trap-door leading to the attic and a part of the roof blew away.

There was pandemonium in our house and it was a battle as to who cried the louder. Some of us disappeared under the beds. Maman, no doubt inwardly shaking, had to console everyone while Papa went into the attic to investigate the extent of the damage. He reappeared with his hair standing on end due to the force of the wind blowing in the attic. There was quite a lot of damage to the roof and he had to wait for morning light to assess the full extent.

Poor Papa, who already had so many jobs to do, now had the roof to repair as well. It was a job which must be done at once as daylight had shown that a quarter of the roof had blown away, most of the tiles now littering the garden. Accompanied by Jean and David he went to town to buy new tiles. They were delivered that day, but the tiles had to be transferred from the door, where they were piled, to the attic.

Papa called on his troops. Everyone in our home who was capable of holding a tile was lined up and drilled. Starting at the door, then at strategic places all the way up to the attic ladder, we were deployed with Maman as the final receiver.

The operation started, tile after tile passed from hands to hands until it finally rested safely in the attic. We decided on a song to speed things along, so to the tune of *Il était un petit navire* the tiles went on their way. When the last tile had been moved up to the attic the girls helped Maman clear the house of dust. Then it was biscuits and chocolate for everyone including the younger looker-ons.

Meanwhile Papa repaired the roof. Munching, we went in the garden, we could see his head sticking out of the hole in the roof as he fixed the tiles. Now and again 'bloodys' were heard, and we had a lot of sympathy for Papa; the nasty storm had given him so much unwelcome work.

Jean was in the attic helping. I would have loved to have been there too. It was men's work and I was a girl, I helped with babies, washed dishes, swept floors, made beds, but men's work was men's work. As I have already said we never encroached on each other's tasks.

Chapter Thirteen

Our village boasted a football team, of which I had been completely unaware until one day Papa announced that he had put his name down for the veteran's game. This game was played at the end of the summer every year apparently, but Papa probably had never felt he qualified for the term 'veteran' up to now.

When we heard Papa saying that he was playing football for the village team, veteran or not, we were delighted. 'We' meaning those of us old enough to understand what twenty-two men running across a farmer's field were doing. Jean and David, having ascertained first that they would be permitted to watch the game, were almost delirious with excitement, while we three girls looked forward to the day of the game for different reasons. Therese, who had discovered that boys were more than little brothers whose noses one wiped, as a possible place of rendezvous with her boyfriend. Madeleine and I for the new experience. Whatever our motives were, one thing we had in common was that we fully expected Papa to be on the winning side.

One Sunday afternoon Papa left the house, making for the village dressed in shorts and tee-shirt. It was rather funny to see him dressed like this. Almost as if, in what we regarded to be his old age, he had once again decided to dress like a boy.

The five of us who had been permitted to view left the desolate younger ones and made our way to the football field; a farmer's field from which the cows had been moved out for the duration of the game. A piece of string between two poles showed the spectators where they were to view from.

The team arrived from the village. The men were dressed in a variety of cloths, some looking as if they belonged to the rag bag. Some of the men even wore hats. Despite their odd looks the team was cheered wildly as it went on to the field.

We found ourselves a nice spot at the top corner of the field, by the make-shift goal post; three pieces of wood making a frame and no net. We sat on the grass waiting for the entertainment to begin and ready to cheer Papa who we felt sure would score many goals.

The village constable was the referee so one thing was certain; the game rules would be adhered to with the law in charge.

The game started amid wild cheering. Why people were cheering already I didn't know, except perhaps that they felt it was a memorable moment in the village's life. Our eyes, of course, were on Papa and judging by the shouts of "Go on David!" coming from the crowd, we were not the only ones following Papa's moves.

Running, Papa was splendid, he was here, there and everywhere. Scoring alas, was another thing, Papa always seemed to be running in the wrong direction. Jean and David yelled "Come on Papa" until they were hoarse. When the final whistle blew Papa was a member of the beaten team, he walked up to the corner where we sat, very despondent and muttering to himself his usual incantations of "Houly, houly, houly."

When Papa joined us David queried, "Why did you not win?" This caused more houly, houly, houlies from our parent. We understood, having lived long enough with Papa to get the meaning of the phrase. Papa could not account for being on the losing side; he, the sportive Englishman! 'Houly, houly, houly!'

We returned home walking across the fields. Maman and the younger children were in the garden. We walked as a silent group. It must have been obvious to Maman that we had nothing to rejoice about. She said to the defeated Papa, "Someone has to lose!" This did not cheer him, he went indoors and disappeared into the loft. Later he came down still morose, he spruced himself and left for the celebration drink at the village hall, Chez Fabry, where both teams and their supporters had arranged to meet.

It must have been the middle of the night when I was awakened by sounds of singing. At first I did not know where I was, but as I became fully aware I recognised the song and the singer; it was Papa singing his favourite song – *It's a Long Way to Tipperary* – I liked the tune of the song which at the time I did not understand. But just now I wanted to sleep and Papa was singing too loud.

Maman came into our room to check that we were all asleep. My wide opened eyes met hers. She put a finger on her lips and whispered to me, "Try to go back to sleep, it's only Papa who has had a bit too much to drink."

I whispered back, "Throw him outside." After all, if the cat made noises during the night, out he went.

Maman gave a little laugh and left the room. I put my pillow over my ears. If that's how Papa celebrates when he loses I hope he never wins, was my last thought before I slept again.

The next day, as far as I was concerned, the Veteran's Football Match became very much something of the past because something momentous happened to me.

Alongside the Chateau was a farm. There, every day, we went to buy milk. We were all eager to take our turn doing this chore. The farmer was very friendly. Depending on the time of the year we received gifts of fruit of whatever kind was in season; cherries and plums, apples and pears or greengages, it was a lovely treat for us. In the winter it was a large cup of chocolate which would be offered. So going for the milk was a task we looked forward to. The farmer had four sons and five daughters, two of the girls were at school with us, the others were older.

That day it was I who was sent for the milk and one of their sons, who we referred to as 'the good-looking one', took notice of me. He declared, with apparent sincerity, "This is the girl I am going to marry," he gave me a lovely smile, a peck on the cheek and a pat on the head. And I . . . promptly fell in love. His name was Alain, even his name I felt was something to love. Of course, little girls are always falling in love with all sorts of things: dolls, cuddly toys, babies, their father, their teachers. Me, I had a real romance, I went home carrying the milk, my head in the clouds. Alain loved me and of course I loved him, it was a beautiful feeling.

I awaited the next evening when I would possibly see Alain again, even if it meant giving my best marbles to bribe whoever was chosen to collect the milk that evening. I said nothing about my 'love affair' either to Maman or Madeleine. It was rather a worry having to keep secrets, but I felt very self-conscious and rather mixed up. Of course, the main fear I had was that I would be laughed at, and possibly Maman might say "Don't be silly" – I could not face that, I did not feel silly. I carried my love inside my young heart through the following weeks. As often as possible I went for the milk, if I caught a glance of Alain I went home feeling happy. He did not repeat his remarks nor, I must admit, did he look my way very often. Well! Perhaps he was shy.

Autumn was nearly over when I heard that Alain was going to be married! I felt betrayed after what he had said to me! I did not want to see him again and I avoided going for the milk. They could keep their fruit and chocolate drinks; me, I was disgusted. They could keep their falling in love for themselves, the grown-ups, that was the end of love for me!

Then one day a girl at school put in my hand a small medal which her brother had sent for me. "Will you be his girlfriend?" she asked. I took the medal and suddenly felt glad that my grown-up 'love affair' was over. It was much nicer to be a little girl once again.

"Thank your brother and tell him I will think about it," was my answer. Love wasn't for me at the moment, but thinking about it was nice!

Village children, it may be thought, live restricted lives. From my experience the reverse is more appropriate. Their involvement in the manifold facets of life is very deep. The people of the village are all very real to them. Some are liked, some are disliked, but no one is a nonentity, all have their own characteristics which the children in the small world of a village are quick to recognise. Life for us at No. 6, Sous-le-Chateau was like a kaleidoscope which we examined closely. No happening was deemed to be unimportant, the older we were the more interested we became. From our parents we received constant care and discipline, slowly we were guided to take a place in society.

As we became older Maman insisted that we looked around our neighbourhood and whenever possible that we gave a hand to those less fortunate than us.

"Who do you mean?" Therese would say, who always complained that she was deprived if she wasn't wearing the latest fashion.

"The old people, and the sick and the very poor," Maman would answer.

I, who wanted patent leather shoes like my cousin Suzette in Verviers, was wondering if anyone could be poorer than me.

"Look around you," said Maman, "you will see what I mean."

At school we were members of a children's organisation called 'The Crusaders'. One of the aims of the organisation was that we did good deeds. Up to then my good deed card had been filled with the jobs I did at home. But now Maman told us to look around us, so we did and soon realised that helping others, as well as being a commendable deed, was also an interesting pastime.

We did not have to look very far. In one of the cottages lived a family where the father never worked and the mother was a very helpless person. At the time the family had three young children and soon a fourth was expected. Therese, once she had done the jobs expected of her at home, was quite happy to go to the cottage and give 'advice' to the helpless lady. The lady regarded Therese as a godsend. Therese, of course, brought all the problems home for Maman to solve.

At the last cottage of the row lived an old lady who was, more than anything else, lonely. When Maman was a young girl, this lady had been amongst the wealthier members of the village's community and had had a reputation for her autocratic overbearing manner. She was now very old, obese and confined to a chair positioned near the window.

She lived with her son, her husband having left her many years ago. We often went in the evening to spend some time with her. The fact that her son had bought her a radio was, of course, a great inducement, for at that time we had no radio. Therese was very fond of music and had a fascination for the box which produced such delightful sounds.

Between those two neighbours we discharged all our 'obligations', as we regarded them, in the cause of good deeds. Of course, such involvements in neighbour's lives brought about situations both tragic and comical.

The lady who Therese had taken under 'her care' gave birth to her baby and was bedridden. It was to Therese that the family looked for help. She went to the house very early in the morning to wash, dress and feed the children and this before she left for school. Therese loved babies and she became very fond of the new-born baby, she was quite happy to look after the new addition to our neighbour's household.

The baby was frail. One day Therese found the lady very distressed and the tiny baby very poorly. She picked the baby up and gently nursed him and in her arms the little baby died. Therese put the baby in his cot and went home to fetch Maman, then having done all she could she returned home and broke down in tears. Maman was very proud of Therese, of the way she kept her head in a time of real crisis.

A few years later, Therese, who was then working in town, met the husband of the lady whose baby she had nursed, the family having moved from the cottage soon after the baby's death. She learned that the lady had also died. Therese received her first proposal of marriage, she was then nearly sixteen. The lady's husband, a rather simple man, saw in the young girl who had helped his family a prospective step-mother for his motherless children. Therese was very upset when she told Maman of the proposal, in fact she was almost in tears. "I did not have to say yes," she said to Maman.

"Of course not," said Maman, "you don't marry for pity, you marry for love, so don't worry about anything, you did right to refuse."

Looking very sad Therese added, "Poor man! he looked so sad." Then finally, as if to convince herself, added, "I am too young to get married anyway."

"Much too young," remarked Maman.

While Therese did such splendid work with such unexpected results, I was more concerned with the old lady who found in me a very attentive audience as she reminisced on her past life and love. She sat in her chair, a mountain of flesh with at least three quivering chins. Above her, on the wall, was a large portrait of an austere man; her runaway husband.

I sat at her feet on the carpet listening to her love story, my young romantic mind seeing a marvellous ending to the tale. I hoped that the day when her runaway husband came charging in to reclaim her love I would be there to witness the emotional reunion of the two parted lovers.

The portrait on the wall was of a rather forbidding man dressed in a fashion of long ago. I did not see the actual situation of an old lady reminiscing about an equally old man, rather I saw Romeo and Juliet. The sleeping beauty and her prince charming. It did not matter that the old lady and I lived in different worlds, we did a lot of good for each other: The old lady had her reminiscences and memories of past happiness, I had my youthful dreams, and somewhere the two met.

Later on, when Therese worked in town, Madeleine joined me in doing good deeds. The old lady always provided us with the opportunity, for if she caught sight of us going past her cottage she called us over. Madeleine had one failing, she was a giggler, once she had a fit of giggles she could not stop herself. One day the old lady called us over to her window for a chat. Madeleine was barely tall enough to reach the window-sill but nonetheless she spent time with me cheering up the old lady by listening to her complaints which were about her health, her loneliness and the loss of her husband, in that order.

One day she was describing her numerous symptoms when suddenly she put out her tongue and made it dance in her mouth to show us how it was now behaving. Madeleine, at once thrown into a fit of giggles, vanished under the window. I stood there trying very hard not to laugh, not at the old lady but at Madeleine and her quick reaction. I was wishing that I, too, could disappear under the window for my sister's face was so contorted that I found it difficult to keep a straight face. Suddenly, I burst out laughing. The old lady forgot her tongue, "Are you laughing at me?" she asked furiously.

All I could think of as an answer was, "Madeleine is tickling me."

"Don't lie, you naughty girl, I know you are laughing at me."

She closed her window firmly in my face. For a few days afterwards we dared not go past her window. On our way to school we crawled along the walls of the cottage and went past her house bent double to avoid being seen. We soon forgot our fears and she soon forgave us. She called us over as usual and we chatted with her and kept her company as we had done before. Then on our weekly 'crusader' card we could once again list our good deeds.

Therese left school in July and she was now being trained as a dispenser in a wholesale chemist. She loved her work and enjoyed the company of her work-mates who were mostly older than her. As a sign that she now regarded herself an adult she had given us her toys.

Music interested her even more than before, if that was

possible. Her friends at work went to the theatre, plays and even to the Conservatory of Music where recitals of famous composers works were given. My sister felt rather the odd one out when discussions on musical tastes took place and so for some time she carried on a campaign in our home directed towards the acquisition of a radio.

We listened to her conversation with Maman on that subject hoping that Therese would be successful in convincing our mother that the lack of a radio was to be deplored. For the time being it looked as if it would be a long time before the sound of music was heard in our home.

Chapter Fourteen

Some dreams come true. One day Therese brought home a newspaper given to her by one of her friends. In this newspaper was a half-page advertisement concerning what was described as a 'miracle' in radio. The advertisement showed the drawing of a radio under the caption 'miracle', and it described all the desirable attributes of the said miracle.

Maman read the article. The cost of the miracle radio was about a fifth of the cost of a radio at the time. Cheap although it was, it was still more than we could afford. The radio was offered on weekly payments. Up to then this was something Maman had avoided, her views being that one bought what one could afford. Therese won her over by reminding her that, as she was now working, we were better off, and offered to put some of her pocket money towards payments. She had looked around her when she proposed this, quickly we older ones agreed to deprive ourselves of sweets and chocolates except, it was just as quickly declared, the chocolate to spread on our bread at breakfast.

Maman was agreeable so we joined the never-never people by ordering the 'miracle' radio. As it was only a fortnight to Christmas we wrote a large urgent letter; it was sent off and, looking forward to our 'miracle', we waited for the post impatiently.

Our patience was sorely tried for it was Christmas Eve when the parcel was delivered, and we saw the 'miracle'. Maman immediately fixed a plug to the wire and we waited with baited breath for the first sounds of melody. Alas . . . instead . . . hissing noises issued from the set. The radio set, a small bakelite box with a cardboard face and two small knobs, which held all our hopes of a musical Christmas and New Year season, besides giving out hissing noises also gave tingling sensations when the knobs were touched. Maman was immediately aware that here was potential danger and much to our disappointment she put it aside for Papa to look at.

Therese arrived home first and on hearing of the arrival of the radio set made a beeline for it. Despite Maman's protests she turned the knobs back and forth, now and then there was a snatch of music then hissing and whistling noises, it was most frustrating. When Papa arrived home he could not adjust the set. Therese did not easily give up. That Christmas Eve, until the time came to leave for midnight Mass, hissing and whistling noises were heard in our living-room. Jean really put his finger on it when he declared, "Well, the radio has arrived, all we need now is the miracle!" It really looked that way.

Christmas Day we were very dejected. Papa went away and was soon back with the village electrician who had agreed to come and fix our new radio set. He took a look at it and exclaimed, "Gracious, where did you get that from?"

Therese explained about the miracle advertisement.

"The only miracle will be if this thing ever works at all!" he declared.

A great sigh was heard when we, as one, showed our disappointment.

Monsieur Debrez, the electrician, went to his van and soon was walking back to our house carrying a radio set. This was no bakelite box, it was a lovely radio set with chromium bars over the loudspeaker.

"There," he said, "I will leave you this for the Christmas holidays."

By the time the holidays were over the sounds of music were so appreciated in our house that Papa went to see his 'bank manager' who also happened to be the baker. The new radio was our first real luxury, for it was dear, but its cost was soon forgotten as it gave so much pleasure. We all had our favourite programmes and for Papa they were those on the English stations. Therese never tired of twisting the knobs to listen to the world coming to our home via the airwaves. The new radio was fun for all.

It was one day to announce shocking news but that was in the future, for the time being we enjoyed the new acquisition.

Christmas and New Year were over, the winter that year really started in January and it was a severe one. There was much snow and the barometer was going down and down as each day passed. Whenever the sun shone we were allowed to play outside making snowballs and snowmen. The pond was frozen but we had not yet tried the ice, Maman having forbidden us all to go near it.

One day Uncle George, who had been ill all that year, came to visit us. I did not understand how my uncle was ill, to me to be ill meant one stayed in bed. I had heard Maman remark to Papa that Uncle George was 'a bit like a child now'. We were playing in the snow when we first caught sight of him and we saw that he was making for the pond.

Jean shouted, "Uncle George, no one has tried the ice yet!"

Uncle George gave us a wave, ran down to the pond and the next thing we knew he was sinking into the water, the ice had broken.

I ran home to call Maman, shouting, "Come quickly, Uncle George is drowning."

Maman ran out of the house to the pond as fast as she could and helped Uncle George out of the water. Madeleine and myself were crying as we watched the rescue. Then we watched our Uncle, his clothes dripping, his teeth chattering, being led by Maman into our house.

Soon he was comfortably settled, draped in blankets, by the stove with a drink of whisky in his hand. He looked very funny huddled there with all the children gathered around him. David spoke first, "Did the ice break Uncle George?"

Then Rene asked, "Why did you fall in the pond?"

Jean said gravely, "He isn't wise."

Of that Uncle George took notice. "Listen children, I did it for you really, now you know the pond is not safe yet." Then addressing himself to Maman, "Better me than them Renee, don't you agree?"

"Better still trying it first with a brick, George," said Maman wisely. "You'll be lucky if you don't put yourself in bed getting chilled like that," she added.

"Oh well," concluded Uncle George, "I'll know better for next year."

The pond froze solid and we were able to use our sleigh on it, but I could not forget how I had felt when Uncle George had disappeared into the water, at the slightest cracking noise I ran off the pond and begged my brothers and sisters to come off too.

Then one morning there was no question of either going to school or playing outdoors. Six of us were coughing our heads off. The doctor was called and confirmed what Maman had already suspected, she had six children suffering from whooping-cough, enough to set up a hospital.

Aunt Miou came to help Maman. All those with the infectious illness were moved into one room. The three youngest children who had escaped the epidemic were kept well away from those infected. At first we were very ill. Maman went from one to the other as the attacks of coughing made us sick. She must have been run off her feet! When the worst of the illness was past, the books that Grandfather had given us long ago went from bed to bed. We never tired of looking through them between bouts of coughing which grew less and less frequent as time passed.

Maman spent a lot of time amusing us. She taught us some old songs; she sang about 'the pilot who did not return from his flight, leaving his son an orphan' or about 'the little girl whose name was "flower of misery" ' and 'the little orphan boy who had to sell his beloved toy soldiers'.

She had a sweet voice and despite the sadness of the songs we were spellbound. And, of course, she told us many stories; those about her youth and about the last war being the most interesting ones. In the evenings it was Papa who came to our bedside, we would ask for more songs. He only knew English songs so he taught us the words of *It's a Long Way to Tipperary* and of *Who's Your Lady Friend*.

When we were fully recovered and back at school I told Sister Marie that I was able to sing in English. At the next school concert I was sent on stage to sing my own version of *Who's Your Lady Friend* which I sang as 'Who's your leggy friend', no one knew at the time, either what the song was about or what I was singing, but Sister Marie was quite pleased that one of her pupils sang in a foreign language.

Papa attempted to teach us English, naturally. We learned small phrases like 'pass the sugar' or 'sit up at the table' and we could all say 'merry Christmas'. On the whole we lacked enthusiasm, despite Maman assuring us that one day we would regret not being bi-lingual. She wasn't being prophetic, rather she was practical, for we had a real opportunity with Papa being more than willing to teach us.

We did not know that one day she would be proved right . . . the future kept its secrets.

Chapter Fifteen

One Sunday morning in May, Maman gave birth to her last baby. To everyone's delight it was a baby girl.

Very early that Sunday morning the 'Lady-with-the-suitcase' and Aunt Miou were in charge of our home and we were all told to go downstairs. Papa took charge of us but it would be true to say that we took charge of him, at least it seemed like that to me.

Therese and I made the breakfast quite amiably for once. We melted chocolate to spread on bread for us and we cooked Papa his English breakfast of bacon and eggs. Then the older ones got ready to attend Holy Mass at the village church. We went to Mass as a group; the time was only seven-thirty. For Madeleine it proved rather an ordeal because her shoes had been left upstairs and it was with a pair of mine that she shuffled up to the village. In church the shoes kept falling off her feet as she knelt. Of course, she felt that everyone laughed at her predicament. She attended the service in her stocking feet. She kept looking at me for help, but what could I do except pick up her shoes and hope no one was looking. We were glad to get back home.

At nine o'clock Aunt Miou sent Papa to telephone for the doctor. This sent alarm through our home – Maman was ill! We waited around very worried, Papa worse than anyone.

At nine-thirty the doctor arrived and went upstairs, but not before patting our anxious faces and assuring us that, "Maman is going to be all right."

At ten o'clock we had a new sister. When the doctor came down he said, addressing himself to us children, "You must all be good, your mother needs a lot of rest."

The morning passed with the young ones in the garden playing while we waited to see our new sister, 'we' meaning the three girls.

Aunt Miou called us upstairs at eleven o'clock. After reminding us to be very quiet she guided us to the cradle beside Maman's bed. In the cradle our one hour old sister lay asleep, brown haired and pretty of face. We were very happy to meet the new addition to our family.

I looked at Maman, she was very sleepy. She whispered, "You can give the baby a name."

Downstairs, while we waited, we had discussed names and particularly girls names, for we felt that this time surely our wishes for a sister would come true. So the three of us had put our heads together and agreed on names for a baby girl. We gave the baby the names of Anne-Marie, Marguerite, Elizabeth, Renee. Lying cosily in her cradle she slept unaware of her three sisters' happiness as they glanced at her.

Somehow we kept the house going that day. We made dinner following Aunt Miou's advice. The roast was probably overcooked, the potatoes undercooked but the white sauce for the garden peas was just right for I was already an expert at sauces.

Therese took charge of Maman's purse which she carried in her pocket and when the ice-cream van came around, as it did every Sunday, she declared that we had to save money for our new sister so there would be no ices today. The younger boys ranged themselves at the garden gate and watched the ice-cream van disappear with tears in their eyes. By evening there was a pile of nappies to be washed and Maman asked me to do them, I did as asked and felt very grown-up to be trusted with such a task.

We muddled through the day, there always seemed to be something which needed attention. It was Madeleine who, although small enough to have to be put to bed, gave herself the task of getting the younger ones ready for bed, and she coped very well; ordering the boys around like a small policeman. Her manner had the right effect for there were no problems.

And so the day of the arrival in this world of Anne-Marie, the last baby to be born into our family, came to an end. Although her first day meant no playing, much housework and a pile of nappies for us girls, it was nonetheless a very happy one. We had a new sister and already she was dearly loved by all.

The following day Papa and Therese left for work as usual and I was put in charge of the house. I had to be up early, something I wasn't too keen on, and send everyone to school. As I already

Marguerite and Jean at Solemn Communion, 1935.

Marie-Therese, bridesmaid to her cousin, 1938.

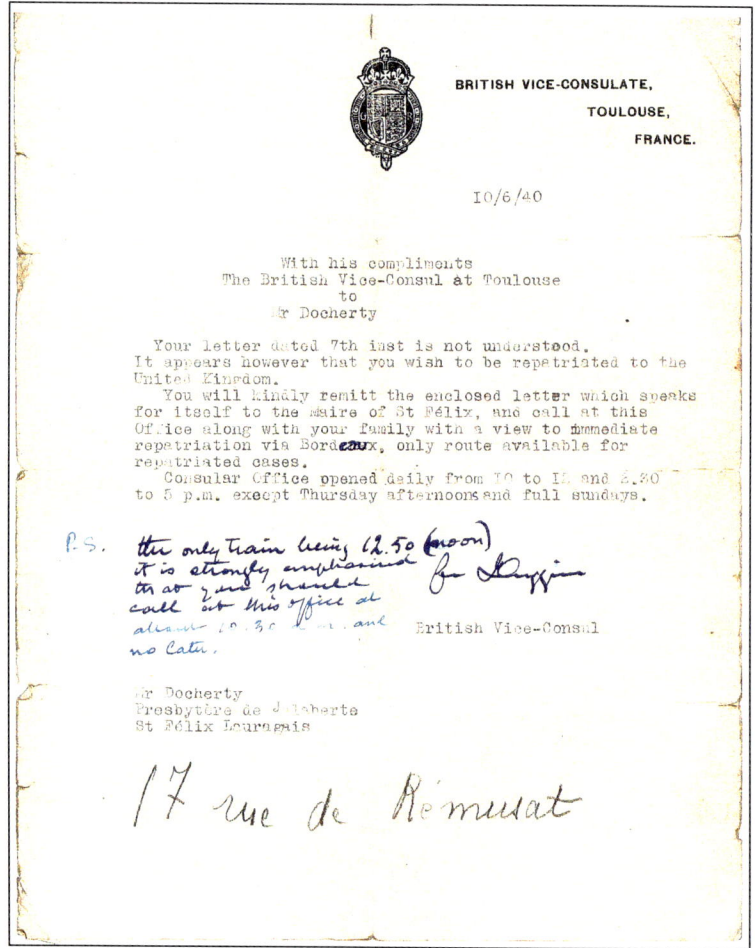

BRITISH VICE-CONSULATE,
TOULOUSE,
FRANCE.

10/6/40

With his compliments
The British Vice-Consul at Toulouse
to
Mr Docherty

Your letter dated 7th inst is not understood.
It appears however that you wish to be repatriated to the
United Kingdom.
You will kindly remitt the enclosed letter which speaks
for itself to the Maire of St Félix, and call at this
Office along with your family with a view to immediate
repatriation via Bordeaux, only route available for
repatriated cases.
Consular Office opened daily from 10 to 12 and 2.30
to 5 p.m. except Thursday afternoons and full Sundays.

P.S. the only train being 12.50 (noon)
it is strongly emphasised
that you should
call at this office at
about 10.30 a.m. and
no later.

British Vice-Consul

Mr Docherty
Presbytère de Roberts
St Félix Lauragais

17 rue de Rémusat

Letter from the British Consulate in Toulouse to
David Docherty concerning arrangements for repatriation
of himself and family to England via Bordeaux.

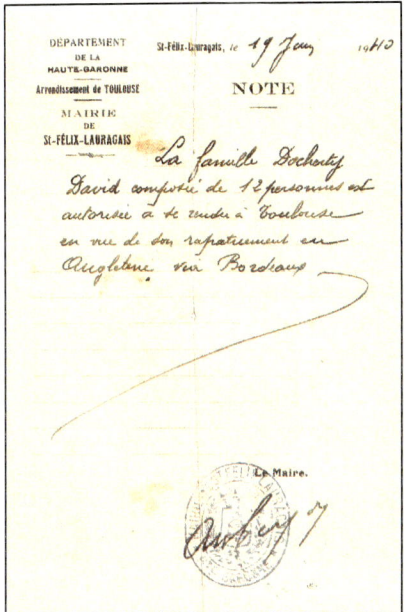

'The Docherty family (David) comprising 12 persons is authorised
to make their way to Toulouse with the view of repatriation
in England via Bordeaux.'

The old presbytery of La Jalabertie, near Toulouse,
where the Docherty family take refuge.

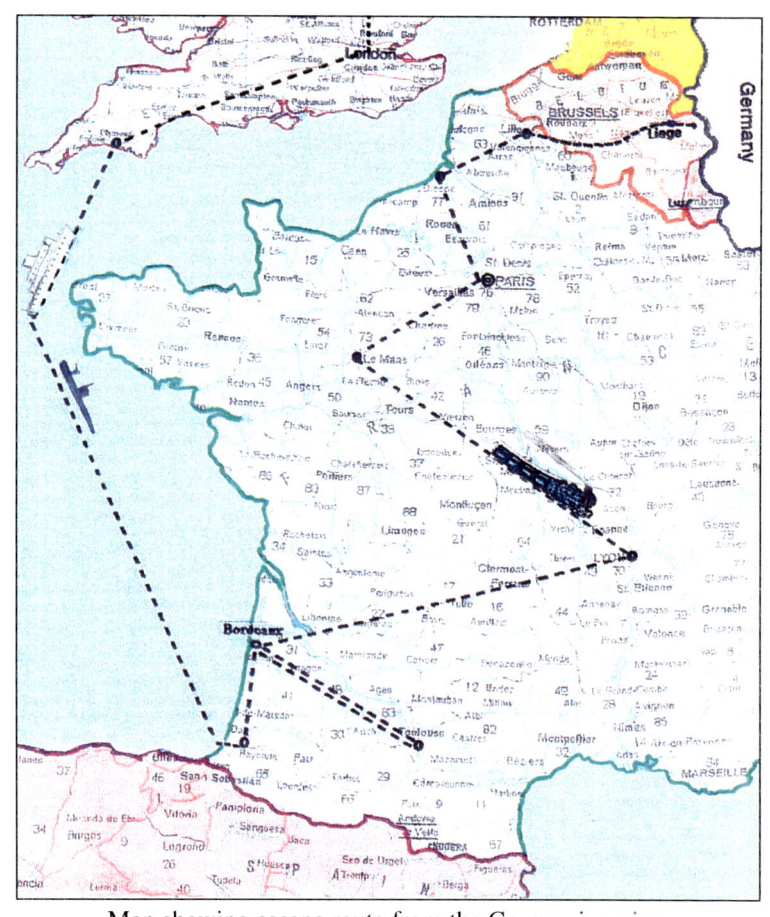

Map showing escape route from the German invasion.

helped in the home, my elevation to the post of housekeeper wasn't as traumatic as it might have been. Poor Maman, who could have done with complete rest, had to act as my adviser. It seemed natural for me to take all my problems to her bedside.

The children finally went away to school, satchels and homework having finally been located as well as clean blouses and clean socks – matching, I'm glad to say. My next job where they were concerned, was to make sandwiches and coffee at lunch-time and take it to the school.

The 'Lady-with-the-suitcase' came to see to Maman's and the baby's needs. Downstairs I surveyed my domain, did some tidying then decided that a book would be more interesting. However, our ever kind neighbour Madame Jacquemin appeared to clean the house. Personally I felt that I was on holiday – not an unusual feeling perhaps as I really ought to have been at school. I would love to say that I was a great help to Maman but I must be truthful, I was of some help and did the minimum of work.

Aunt Flore, Maman's sister-in-law, on holiday in the village at the time, came over and it was due to her that the work was done.

One morning Maman asked me to cook her some prunes. Prunes were then rather expensive. I went shopping and bought the prunes. Back at home I followed Maman's directions and put the prunes on to cook. "Let them simmer," said Maman. I let them simmer and returned to my book. Then realising it was almost lunch-time I rushed around preparing the sandwiches and the coffee for the scholars. Even Pierre, barely two years old, was at school, the nuns having accepted kindly to take care of him.

I ran all the way to school, the coffee jug spilling as I went as fast as possible. At school I then had a nice chat with Sister Marie who enquired about the new baby and Maman. Finally I returned home.

As I walked in the house Maman's voice, coming from upstairs, could be heard urgently saying, "Maggie, Maggie, what's burning . . ?"

Oh my goodness! The prunes . . . was my immediate thought. I opened the living-room door, the room was blue with smoke.

"I have burned the prunes," I shouted to Maman.

"Take them off the stove and open the window," she replied.

I did as I was told. Then putting a towel around the hot pan, I took the prunes up to Maman with tears streaming down my face.

Maman shook her head, looking at me with reproach, "Where have you been?"

Remembering my chat with Sister Marie, I looked at the floor and shed more tears, I knew I was wrong to have stayed away so long.

"Go downstairs and get me a fork," said Maman.

The fork in her hand she carefully picked out the prunes which were still edible. Watching my poor mother eating the burnt prunes I cried even more.

When I went downstairs again I tried to atone by doing some ironing – thank goodness the clothes were sent to a laundry in town for I fear we would have been wearing clothes unfit to be seen in. Then I made a good cup of coffee which I took up to Maman to make up for the loss of the prunes.

"Oh well!" sighed Maman, when she saw me, "you do your best. Try to keep your mind on the work and all will be well."

I tried to remember that piece of advice and heaved a big sigh of relief when Maman came downstairs with 'little Anne' as we called her.

Jean and I were chosen as godparents and one day, with Aunt Miou, we made our way to church for the Christening. This wasn't unusual as children were often chosen as godparents. I wanted to carry the baby but wasn't allowed and felt rather cheated for, after all, I had washed her nappies! Surely that made me old enough . . . that was my reckoning anyway. But those who knew better than me had other ideas so, with Jean, I put my hand on our new sister's tiny hands as we affirmed on her behalf during the ceremony.

Afterwards our home settled back to normal life with Maman once more at the helm.

Meanwhile Madeleine had been very busy, she had washed and ironed all the linen in her doll's pram in readiness for her baby sister, whom she expected to take the place of her doll. She was disappointed when she was told that the baby was too small to play with, and it was very sadly that she put the pram away. To make up for all the disappointment, at night when the baby was ready for bed we were allowed a period of holding our sister on our laps for a while. None of the girls missed that moment, it was so nice to have a baby sister. The boys looked and only Pierre and Fernand came near, but there was no jealousy from them for the little sister who received all the family's attention; except perhaps Pierre who never ceased to repeat that he was 'nice', to be quickly assured by whoever he addressed that remark to, "Yes, you are very nice."

As for Papa, he was once again doing what we called 'his marching act'. At night, if the baby was crying he would pace the bedroom floor with the baby snugly over his shoulder. He hummed a marching song softly. He had done this so many times that we knew the tune by heart, and every baby who had received this treatment obviously enjoyed the singing and the marching as while he walked and sang, peace reigned, and when he stopped the baby cried.

It always seemed to me that baby Anne had more of this treatment than the other babies before her. Perhaps I did not sleep as soundly as I had done now that I was one of the 'older girls'. Babies, as much as I loved them, put years on me . . . what with nappies and burnt prunes and being a godmother!

Chapter Sixteen

We were sitting on the lawn with Maman one Sunday afternoon. The village fair and the Fête were over for another year.

Our Sunday mornings were taken by Holy Mass attendance and making the Sunday lunch plus the usual chores, and of late Madeleine and I baked cakes and the cakes were what we discussed on the lawn with Maman.

On Sundays, weather permitting, many town-dwellers came up to the village for walks. Walking being then a favourite pastime for sunny and warm days. Sous-le-Chateau, where we lived, was a very pleasant spot where, after climbing the hill from the town, the walkers made a stop; relaxing beside the pond. We had a large garden, only a small part of it was cultivated for vegetables, the front was a rather untidy green.

Therese was the first to suggest, "Why don't we have a tea-garden?"

"Do you realise how much work it would be?" asked Maman, who still had young children. Little Anne the youngest was just one at the time.

"We could run it," the three of us said with one voice.

I added, "I'm sure Jean would help, and David."

"Well," replied Maman, "it's certainly a good idea."

"Oh yes . . . we could have small tables . . . and chairs . . . and umbrellas!" enthused Therese.

"And swings . . ." said Madeleine clapping her hands, then she turned to me. "We could make cakes and sandwiches . . ."

I found this very satisfactory. After all, had Maman not just complimented us on our baking!

The more we talked about the idea the more interesting it became. Therese had a few tries at giving a name to our proposed tea-garden.

Jean had come within ear-shot and followed our conversation for a while. "Papa will soon give it a name when he hears about it, I bet you he will call it 'the blooming place'," was his opinion.

We all laughed but were not deterred. Making an effort, for it was very relaxing sitting in the heat of the afternoon, I stood up: "Come on let's get started . . . we'll clear the front garden to begin with."

We rounded up Papa's garden tools which were always to be found strewn all over the place as all the children played with them. Then we started preparing the ground for what we already called jokingly 'The blooming tea-garden'. We dug and pulled weeds. Barrel loads of those were taken to the pond to be dumped into the water.

Papa was totally unaware of all our activities, he was in his loft caring for his pigeons. We wanted to present him with a *fait accompli*, so we hoped he would not appear in the garden for the rest of the day.

Four of us started on the work . . . soon ten of us were occupied; even little Anne had joined the working gang, picking up weeds to put in the barrow. Clearing the front of the house of grass we made interesting discoveries. A cobbled stone pavement was uncovered all along the front of the house . . . and we unearthed an old well.

We worked hard, Maman made us a picnic to eat on the lawn. We were soon back at work and by evening the front garden was cleared of weeds, grass and stones, and Jean had raked it nice and smooth. We sat relaxing in the cool of the evening. The garden was prepared, all we must get now was the equipment. Jean and David proposed to make small benches. We felt this was a good idea as it would give our tea-garden a rustic touch. So all we needed now were tables and umbrellas – "and swings," said Madeleine.

That afternoon the town visitors had paused to watch us work, we felt certain that they would make our place a stop if we could get the equipment. We were pondering over our problem when Papa came out into the garden to take a stroll, he passed us and wandered leisurely round to the front – we looked at each other!

He wasn't leisurely coming back, in fact it's true to say he was back like a shot. "What's happened to the front garden?" he demanded to know.

We were all wishing Maman was with us, she stood up well to Papa's wrath. She was indoors now with Therese putting the small children to bed. I pushed Madeleine forward for she normally got away with everything short of murder, and Papa looked angry and needed placating. Bravely she announced:

"We are making a tea-garden."

We all waited with apprehension.

"A blooming what?" snapped Papa.

"A blooming tea-garden," said Jean, almost spelling the words, he added, "to make some money."

Oh! that's good, I thought, the money making might appeal to Papa. I said timidly, "We only need tables and umbrellas now."

Papa looked at me as if I had announced the end of the world.

"In my blooming garden!" he was almost livid. Looking at every one of us in turn he declared passionately, "There will be no bloody tea-garden here, I blooming well tell you."

Papa's garden was sacred, obviously, and he made no bones about it. We ran indoors, all very upset.

"What's the matter?" asked Maman.

"Your husband . . . as usual . . ." answered Therese.

"Oh!" said Maman summing it all up. I shook my head. She knew her husband all right. No meant no and that was that.

So the tea-garden remained just a good idea.

The following Sunday, Papa safely in his loft, we decided that if a tea-garden was objectionable, a nicely laid garden should be acceptable.

"What do you think Maman?" we asked. "Can we have flower gardens and paths."

"Of course," she said, "but don't disturb anything."

It was a lovely warm day, we had our dinner on the table under the greengage trees, as we often did on warm days. After dinner Maman went indoors to read; her favourite pastime on Sunday afternoons. We sat in the garden, spreading ourselves around on the lawn; the elder ones discussing how the garden would look while the younger ones hung around waiting for the work to start. When the midday heat had lessened we all moved over to the front garden. Then Jean and I started drawing patterns on the ground for the flower gardens. We had Grandfather's books for ideas as to how to lay a garden decoratively. We soon realised our limitations, looking at the grandly laid garden, and we finally settled for a circular bed in the middle and four triangular beds around it. We had attempted more elaborate designs but with Madeleine, the boys and little Anne all drawing lines going in various directions, it had resulted in a shambles.

Jean had finally called for order, then he swept the ground clear of all markings, drawing on the ground the final layout. Everyone looked at the pattern which, even though plain, looked quite attractive. "Right, all we need now is soil," pronounced Jean.

We raided the garden and dug soil from everywhere we could think of, then we set down to the task of making a well laid out garden to give a nice frontage to the house.

We took plant cuttings from Maman's flower bed and Jean used his initiative by going to the gardener to ask for 'spare plants'. He was given handfuls. Some of our young friends from the village who had been watching us working went home for tea and returned with plants from their gardens. Soon we had well-stocked flower beds and we were very proud of our work, even the cat sat by as if to admire the newly laid garden. As for Papa, when he saw the garden he said nothing at all. For a while we felt that once again we had a dream garden, until one day . . .

We returned from school at tea-time to find the two little ones, Pierre and Anne, waiting for us at the gate. "Look!" they said pointing at the garden.

There was nothing to see . . . our flower garden had vanished . . . disappeared without a trace. We ran indoors to Maman.

"What happened?" we cried.

Maman was busy making the tea. I think she had expected our reaction for she was almost curt, "Your father needed the soil," she said.

"Needed the soil . . . Oh Maman there is lots of soil in the garden!"

"He wanted the soil, that's all," said Maman.

We went on protesting loudly until Maman said with finality, "I want to hear no more about it."

"Can I ask where the plants are?" I looked at Maman.

She answered, "They are in a pail of water, I rescued them."

And then it dawned on me that she was on our side and she too was upset about the flower-beds.

After tea we went out to plant the flowers alongside the vegetables, and we noticed the big trench . . . it had been dug all along the hedge between the garden and the orchard — Papa, who was once again on strike, had spent the day causing havoc in the garden; first it had been the flower-beds, then the trench!

Madeleine said, shaking her head, "I heard him tell Maman that the roots of the trees from the orchard are taking the goodness from the garden. I think he is going to build a wall inside the ground."

And so he did. He built a wall inside the ground and he built a wall on top of the ground, then proceeded with small walls all over the garden. Uncle Paul, on his visits at our house, called it all the 'fortifications' or 'David's Maginot Line'. We laughed about it all in those days. But the day came when we wished Papa had kept his garden where he did everything Royal Engineer style.

Chapter Seventeen

Three years had passed, I was now fourteen years old. Little Anne was out of the baby stage. Therese was progressing well with her training. Jean went to school in town. Papa had not done much more to the house and apart from the pigeon racing he had given up his sporting activities. In our eyes all he needed was a long white beard . . . we felt that he had reached that stage.

At his place of employment there were still periods of industrial dispute. When this happened Papa, who was now regarded in the village as a very experienced house builder, was employed repairing houses and buildings with a local builder. Once he had been given the task of building a family vault in the cemetery.

Papa was a superstitious person and at first he had not liked the work very much. But as the days passed and he went with the builder to the cemetery to do the work, he relaxed until he could actually joke about it. When he arrived home in the evening he would tell us about his day which now started on arrival at the cemetery with a "Good morning you lay-about," or "Don't answer all at once."

He did quite a lot of work for the builder and as he could not be in two places at once, our home waited for further improvements. Money had to go on more urgent things, as the children were growing up and it cost more to feed and clothe them.

Therese, now in her third year of training as a dispenser, had turned her eyes towards romance and had, unknown to Papa, a steady boyfriend. Maman knew of the romance which was rather like a cloak and dagger affair as it had to be kept from Papa's notice at all costs. He forbade even the thoughts of boyfriends.

We girls had six brothers and that to Papa was a large enough male entourage; the fact that we rather liked to extend our friendships to outsiders was unthinkable to Papa. He frowned on any male friends brought to our home by the boys. I think Papa was the kind of person who would have flourished in a harem with a lot of ladies all to himself.

I left school that year and it was my turn to go to work. Through family connections I got a job at a high class stationer's in town. Another girl called Maria was already employed there. She was older than me and she set about making me into a glamorous lady like herself. I was very happy with the prospect and was soon full of myself. Although my wardrobe for work was limited to mostly sweaters and skirts – I knitted the sweaters and Maman made the skirts – I still regarded myself as very smartly dressed. With a touch of lipstick applied at work from an old lipstick I had pinched from Therese and a bit of burned cork on my eyebrow, I felt that I was irresistible.

I was irresistible, not as I wished it but to the two young nephews of the ladies who owned the shop. It wasn't my looks which were the object of attraction, rather I was ideal as someone to tease. The eldest one was only one year younger than me, but it is marvellous how young thirteen is once one has reached the ripe old age of fourteen. So to me they were only youngsters, hence their incessant teasing to topple me off my self-made pedestal.

Now that Therese and I worked in town, we had become, so she felt, very sophisticated young ladies – one moment we were schoolgirls who ran and skipped and played with toys, the next we left all that for the children. We worked and we earned money, not much at the time, but enough to make us feel that we had left childhood behind.

Maman did her best to keep us dressed in the fashion of the time, she sewed our clothes and in return we helped in the home, for Maman could not do both. To keep abreast of fashion we looked around the smart shops in town and made mental notes of the latest styles, Maman was a very good seamstress and copied from our drawings. Of course, we did not have many clothes so we took good care of what we possessed and made clever use of scarves and belts or even embroidery on dresses.

Therese, although only sixteen, was very much in love and

Maman allowed her, unknown to Papa, to go with her boyfriend to a cinema on Sunday afternoons. But, of course, there was a proviso, she had to have a chaperone . . . It was I who was given the task of playing gooseberry. To my sister, who would have liked total freedom, I was a sore point. Everywhere she went, I went, and despite my veneer of sophistication I was very young at heart; I did not like to be parted from my elder sister. At the cinema, if there were only two seats together, it was I who insisted that I should sit beside my sister, much to the dismay of the young couple and, of course, their feelings towards me were far from friendly.

I took my chaperoning very seriously. My sister seldom had a moment alone with her boyfriend. I think they both must have hated me in those days. Then one day I found a young boy to my liking, fourteen like myself and still at college. I began to look for freedom, but my sister did not forget my vigilance where she was concerned – she reported my 'romance' to Maman who immediately applied her veto: "You are too young for boyfriends," I was told. My pleas that I wanted to get married some day were ignored, I could wait another few years before worrying about finding someone.

Actually, when I was sixteen years old I received two proposals of marriage. One from a young man in the village who regarded me as the ideal person to run a shop he was intending on buying. I took the proposal in all seriousness as was intended, and with the same seriousness refused, explaining that I wanted to marry someone who had a successful business, not an unknown starter. I told Maman of the proposal and of my refusal, she congratulated me on my great expectations but I would have sworn she was laughing. The second proposal was from a nineteen year old boy, son of a factory owner. He proposed to me by letter and issued me with details as to how I could let him know of my acceptance or refusal – by either meeting him outside a cinema in town or not. Maman gave me a job to do the day of the tryst and I forgot all about it, my would-be husband found himself refused unwittingly . . . such is fate.

Once a year, at the end of July, the village fair took place. To the villagers it was three days of relaxation and merry-making. In the centre of the village was 'La Place' as it was called – a kind of village square lined with trees, and where a monument to the

1914-18 war heroes was erected.

There, early in the week preceding the opening of the fair, the romanies arrived, settling themselves and unloading their vans under the eyes of many very excited children. A roundabout, some swings and stalls, plus a shooting gallery, were soon erected around the square. The village authorities saw to the erection of a raised dance floor, and the village centre was completely transformed.

The transformation was heralded by all with anticipation of the good times ahead. To the children the roundabout was the greatest attraction and to a certain extent so were the swing-boats. Then, of course, there were the games for the children and for the grown-ups; the 'auction' and the gaming tables. For three whole days merry-making would be uppermost in everyone's mind. With everything in its place and the fair all set ready for the moment of opening, excitement ran high. Our village had become a festive village and we could hardly wait for the festive sounds of the fairground organ to signify that the fun had started. I must admit that the sounds were a bit drowned by the chuff-chuff of the power-making tractor, which had a heavy cable trailing along the ground, but no one minded or even noticed it after a while.

I was fourteen and for the first time I was allowed to watch and, if I was asked, join in the dancing which took place in the evening. With Jean, I was to act as chaperone for Therese who was old enough now to be on the dance floor and even to sit at one of the small tables dotted around the dance floor where drinks were consumed. Her romance was on the wane but she was hoping that the romance of the night's music and dancing would rekindle its ebbing fire.

The fair opened on the Sunday afternoon. Madeleine and I, with Anne by the hand, followed by Jean leading all his younger brothers, were there to watch the start of the festivities. Each one of us had his own pocket money, not a large sum alas, so much consideration had to be given as to how it was spent. The younger members of the family soon disposed of their share as the gaily turning roundabout claimed them, then they had to resign themselves to watching. But this was something that many children did – watching and . . . waiting, who knows, one's relations might be amongst the crowd and might give one a treat!

The afternoon was fully enjoyed. On the Sunday there were no games – these would take place over the following two days. Madeleine, little Anne and I wandered over to the gaming tables, and I received my first lesson on the folly of gambling . . . The table we stopped at was divided in squares of different colours. All one had to do was choose a colour and put one's money on the table, then a coloured dice was thrown – whatever colour showed uppermost was the winning colour, money was paid to those whose money was laid on the winning square.

"Do you think I dare gamble?" I whispered to Madeleine.

Jean had arrived on the scene and guessed my intention. "Maman would not like it," he remarked.

"Go on," said Madeleine, adding, "Jean would not dare but you would."

At this I felt ten feet tall, so I dared and I put my money on the table – one franc was the minimum stake, this was double my normal pocket money so I was really being rash. The dice was thrown and . . . I won!

"Oh great! You are lucky. Try again," this from Madeleine.

"She would not dare," said Jean.

I dared and I won again.

Jean looked interested, it was him this time who said, "I'll dare you to try again."

I did and . . . I won again! I now had twelve francs in my hand. I had never possessed so much money before. The gambling fever went to my head, I had another go and . . . I lost.

"Have another go," urged Madeleine.

Jean looked disgusted. "You'll lose," he declared.

I had another go and another go until I had four francs left in my hand. By then Madeleine wasn't saying anything anymore and Jean looked contemptuous. I was wishing I had taken notice of him. We left the gambling table.

I had held twelve francs in my hand and I had lost it. I felt a criminal and a fool. What would Maman say?

Back at home later I told her about it, I thought it was better if I told her myself. I knew if I did not speak someone would. Maman gave me the version of – one bird in the hand is worth two in the bush – then she added, "At least it wasn't your money you lost, keep away from the tables next time."

I did. I had learned my lesson. Fancy that I had had twelve francs of my own . . . and had stupidly lost it, it was hard to swallow.

The evening came. The dancing on the open-air dance floor started at seven o'clock and we were there in good time. Therese, who had been a bridesmaid that year, had a lovely long dress and was very pleased with herself. She walked, her head held high, her long blue satin dress making swishing noises as she moved as gracefully as she knew how. I had a lovely peach coloured dress with a gold belt which Maman had made for me. Jean walked alongside his two sisters, I felt that he should have been proud to accompany two girls as smart as I felt we looked but he looked grim. The fact was that he did not relish the task of chaperone, he would rather have spent his evening at the shooting gallery. Watching two girls awaiting invitations to dance was about the worst job he had ever been given.

Walking up to the village, from where strains of music could be heard, I whispered to my sister, "Let's tell Jean that we will all go our own way and meet at the corner at half past ten."

"He will tell Maman," retorted Therese, adding: "You know him once he is told to do something, he does it."

"How much money have you got?" I asked Therese.

My sister thinking that I wanted to borrow from her was cagey. "Why?" she queried.

"If we pay Jean he might go away," I whispered to her. Therese gave me one franc and I added one. Jean was now walking ahead of us so I ran up to him.

"There," I said, putting the two francs in his hand, "you go to the shooting gallery and we'll see you at the corner of the road at half past ten."

Jean's face was beaming, and promptly leaving his two charges he ran ahead of us. Everybody was happy now, I felt. Maman, who thought her two daughters were chaperoned, Jean, who could spend his evening at the shooting gallery and Therese and I who were now free from Jean's surveillance. We looked forward to the evening even more than we had done before.

Therese was dancing every dance, she was happy to find herself so popular. Me, well after all I had not expected to be the 'belle of the ball', I was only fourteen and there was too much competition from the village's older girls. Still I had hoped that someone would find me interesting enough to want to dance with. Standing expectantly I looked around me, the musicians raised stand caught my attention and I spotted a young violinist who looked about my own age.

I went and stood as near as possible to the musician's stand and stared hard at my chosen 'man'. He got the message, for after a short while I saw him whispering to the band leader, then he put down his violin and came over to me and asked me for a dance. This was the first time I had ever been on a dance floor, possibly it was his first time as well for we just seemed to walk around trying hard to keep to the music. Clumsy or not I kept a happy smile on my face. Soon we were on first names, he was Jean-Claude and he was fifteen and I felt very happy to have his attention. We danced a few times together, I had never thought anything could be as exciting. I forgot Therese and I forgot Jean and the time until I felt my arm being touched during an interval.

Jean was beside me. "Where's Therese? It's time to go home," he said.

He was about the last person I wanted to see. I was enjoying myself and home was the last place I wanted to go at the moment.

"Come on," urged Jean, "let's find Therese."

Reluctantly I left the dance floor and followed Jean.

A group of village boys came up to us.

"Mademoiselle Docherty, I take it?" one of them said to me.

I knew he was making fun of me so I ignored him, but he would not be ignored.

"Would you follow me Mademoiselle Docherty?"

"Leave me alone," I said furiously. I had no time for village boys today. After all, had I not just danced with the interesting violinist who had treated me like the young lady I felt that I was. I had left my childhood behind and I did not want anyone to make fun of me. Of course, in my eyes I was now a real 'Mademoiselle' but not as a term of derision in the way the boys meant it.

The boys in the group were whispering amongst themselves and laughing. Then one of them said, "Go to the corner bar, there's something you should see," and another added:

"Your Papa wants you."

"Come on," said Jean, "better go and see what Papa wants."

We ran to the bar, rather surprised for as far as we knew Papa had no interest in the village fair. When we arrived at the bar I lost all my pretensions – Papa was inside the bar, standing in the middle of the floor, a glass of beer in his hand and singing at the top of his voice, obviously very drunk . . .

Jean and I stood there dumfounded, that bar had a rather unsavoury reputation and our Papa was inside – drunk and singing – we did not know which was the worse.

"Oh dear," said Jean, shaking his head, "our family is disgraced!"

"Oh yes," I sighed, "we are disgraced! What will Maman say?"

Then I remembered Therese who was dancing unaware that everyone was laughing at Papa. There were only a few people in the bar but to me everyone must know by now what Papa was doing. Never mind being grown-up anymore and having danced with a violinist. All my happiness had evaporated. Our Papa sang in shady bars . . . Jean wanted to go inside and drag him out. Really Papa was doing no more than having a bit of fun at the fair, but we applied all our 'mustn'ts' to him.

We left the singing Papa amongst his 'shady' friends and went back to the dance floor to look for Therese. Our sister was found in a crowd of gay young people. I whispered in her ear, "Papa has disgraced the family."

Therese took me aside and I told her what Jean and I had witnessed.

"Oh," cried our sister, "that's dreadful."

One of her friends looked up. "Who's died?" she asked.

Therese did not answer, she turned her back on all her friends. We followed her as she marched quickly back home.

We found Maman sitting in the living-room reading a book; her favourite pastime when the family was settled for the night.

"Your husband has spoiled everything for us," announced Therese.

Maman was used to dramatic announcements, she quietly put away her book and enquired, "My husband, what?"

"He has disgraced us," said Jean and I together.

"Hum," said Maman looking thoughtful. "What has he done?"

We told her.

"That's unforgivable, of course," she pronounced. "Do you all suggest that we lock him out for the night?"

"You are not taking us seriously, are you?" queried Therese.

"Well," said Maman, "I think that your father can look after himself and of course the fair is for him as much as for everyone else."

We were getting nowhere. Jean went to bed and I followed as I was now very tired. Therese could still be heard for a while as she tried to make Maman understand how we felt. Then she too came to bed. She took her lovely long dress off, saying in a rebellious voice, "The next time I go to a dance I am going to get drunk and see what happens."

I don't know what Maman told Papa the following day, but this was the last time we saw him sing in a bar.

As for me, now that I was fourteen and had been to my first dance, I felt very grown-up and worldly-wise! I knew so many things. I was a little mother to my little sister who was my godchild. I was a bread-winner, even although my contribution to house-keeping was very small. One thing I knew most of all was the fear of Hitler. I had heard Uncle Paul say once again to Maman: "You should take the children to England, you know they are unsafe here if there is a war."

Maman had sighed. "The cost of taking them to England is so high we can't afford it, besides where would we live in England?"

So life went on . . . I was going through a phase of having fearful dreams about our home being devastated by war. I said nothing. I felt too old to complain about nightmares, one had them and one forgot them.

After all, morning always came . . .

Chapter Eighteen

When we were children our acquaintance with the world of celluloid, or rather cinema to give it its proper name, was very limited. Sometimes at school we were shown slides. As we depended for this form of entertainment on visiting missionaries the slides showed mostly life in African countries, they gave the school children an opportunity to see how people in those countries lived. It was very interesting at first but repeat showings were boring, for there were no stories as such, just dark coloured people moving, mostly grinning, in front of the screen.

One day we were taken to a town cinema by one of the Sisters of the Convent to see a film show. Therese and I had looked forward to this outing, for it was the first time we had visited a real cinema. And this was conspicuously obvious for the first part of the film show when we sat on what appeared to be very uncomfortable seats – just a bar! We discovered at the interval, when we heard the sound of the seats springing back, that behind us lay the actual seating part. We felt very foolish and we did our best to hide our embarrassment. When a school friend remarked, "Oh, you did not know about the folding seats?" I replied quickly:

"Of course we did, we liked it that way in case there were germs on the seats."

The film on show was entitled *How I Killed My Child*. It was a film with a moral; the reason why the nuns had decided that we should see it. But we were unaware of this. We kept whispering to each other, "Has he been killed yet?" Meanwhile shading our eyes for fear of witnessing the fatal blow or shot, whichever way the child was due to be killed. Enough said to admit that we saw very little of the film.

On our way home with our schoolmates it was obvious that no

one had seen the point of the film. Some girls were saying, almost with regret, "We did not see the child killed."

The next day at school we had to write an essay on the film we had seen.

Therese wrote: 'The film was very clever but we did not see it because we wanted to miss the killing and we looked the other way. We saw Julienne pull Georgette's hair and Andree tried to trip the usherette.' Sister wrote on the essay: 'You will make a good spy, keep watching.'

I wrote: 'It was a very clever film but I did not see it because my sister would not let me.' Sister wrote on my essay: 'Don't tell tales.'

When we told Maman about the cinema visit, she exclaimed, "What a waste of money." And this is how we felt too.

Our next outing to a cinema was to see a film called *The Hunchback*. Maman had wanted us to see this film as she had enjoyed the book very much. Papa left the four elder children at the cinema in town one Sunday afternoon and went to join his pigeon friends. "I'll call for you at the end of the show," was his parting shot.

The film was a riveting dramatic love and adventure story. I nearly spoiled the outing for us. As the cinema manager was going past along the gangway, Therese asked me to enquire of him what time it was. "Half past five," said he.

"What!" I exclaimed. "Is it that late?"

The manager shone his torch on our group.

"Have you been sitting there since this morning?" he asked, looking rather angry, and he added: "I think that you had better go home."

We had only been at the cinema for about an hour and tearfully we assured him that Papa was coming for us at half past six, he relented and left us after bidding us to keep quiet.

Therese turned on me. "Shut your big mouth," she said.

So vulgar, I felt.

I did not speak another word until we got home, except for whispering to Therese, "I'll tell Maman." Alas when we got home Maman was more interested in hearing all about the film.

It was me who set the table for supper, I gave Therese the oldest cup and plate we had, then I dipped my bread in my tea and dropped it on her plate. I knew my sister could not stand the sight of wet bread and in fact she had to leave the table. But she had the last victory when Maman said to me:

"You do the dishes, Therese cannot stand wet bread."

"It's her turn," I murmured.

"Do as I said," replied Maman.

Therese grinned with satisfaction. I could have cried I was so vexed.

Once a travelling cinema visited the village. It was set up on 'La Place' where many villagers congregated in the evening to view a showing of *Romeo and Juliet*. Madame Fadier, Maman's friend, offered to take the four elder children to the evening show. It was a night to remember, but not by what went right, rather by what went wrong!

The source of the power for the working of the projector was elbow-grease. A small man turned frantically at the handle of the large machine, trying to give a sense of continuity to the show. There were paraffin lamps which smoked and gave off obnoxious fumes.

The show had reached the famous balcony scene when suddenly the screen collapsed. When it was righted there was a large tear right across it and the cinema, alas, was declared closed. To make up for what she thought was a disappointing evening for us Madame Fadier had bought us a Japanese flower – a dried up flower which blossomed when put in water – the lady of the ambulant cinema sold the flowers at a small table beside the travelling van.

We had returned home none the wiser as to the Shakespearian tale's denouement but, as we were very young at the time, being out late at night was such an exciting thing that we minded not what Juliet's fate ultimately was.

Then, as previously mentioned, the time came when I was to chaperone Therese and her first boyfriend. I became well and truly acquainted with the world of the cinema. Deanna Durbin, a famous singer at the time, was my favourite. Watching her I found my real calling; I wanted to be a famous singer. Poor Maman had to put up with her daughter attempting to sing in higher octaves than she was capable. One never to be forgotten day I was helping a friend of my mother whose young maid had deserted her. The lady's brother, who lived next door to her, was the village's choir-master and he was in the garden at the back of the house. Wanting to be discovered, while making the beds upstairs, I sang, putting my whole heart into it.

Soon I was rewarded when a knock at the bedroom door turned out to be the lady's brother. My heart jumped with joy, my dream was coming true. I waited . . .

"Could you please make a bit less noise, my little girl is asleep," was all he said.

I didn't think anyone could suffer a bigger blow than I did at that moment. I had much to learn, of course.

Chapter Nineteen

I had spent most of my life in Andrimont, and my contact with the village and its inhabitants was a very close one. I knew everyone by name.

The village itself wasn't very large. Three main streets and the village's square would aptly describe it. The village, which had six shops, a blacksmith and a flour mill, was dominated by the Church of Saint Laurent and the Hotel de Ville. As there were two bakers, one butcher, two pork shops and two grocery stores, the population must have been fairly large to support all those services. There was also one tailor, two hairdressers, two carpenters and a coffin-maker. In fact, the village was almost a self-sufficient community, and it was on the whole a happy one. There were, of course, some feuding families who had at some time in their lives vowed that they would never speak to each other again. They kept to this pledge, thus creating interesting situations as it was difficult to avoid anyone permanently in the village.

Of course, the structure of the village life was a divided one, this because of differing interests. There were farmers and there were industrial workers. The farmers had their fields, their animals, their sowing and harvesting. While the industrial workers had their crafts, their six days a week, their industrial problems; such as strikes and lack of orders at this particular period in history. But still the two sides were friendly and would take a Sunday drink together at the local bars.

Amongst the younger generation there were organisations like the Young Christian Workers and the Young Agricultural Workers. Then there were two dramatic societies, with the interest of the members being reflected in the choice of plays.

And of course there was the Mothers' Union, the president of which was the 'Lady of the Castle', and finally the Church Choir.

We had every reason to be proud of our village, it catered for such a variety of interest that life was never dull. My sister and I were members of the dramatic society and, as in the winter there were many concerts given, we were very much in demand to take parts in the plays. We thoroughly enjoyed the acting and, perhaps even more, the rehearsals, which meant we had a good reason to be out of the house later than usual – this was a very attractive proposition for us. Our many outings were frowned upon by Papa who was very strict regarding the time of our coming in at night time. But as the rehearsals took place at the castle at the time, and Papa had a great regard for the 'Lady of the Castle' who spoke very good English, what could he do but agree when we were asked to take part in yet another concert. We could claim that we were doing it for good causes, which we were really as these events were fund raising occasions as well as ways of passing the long winter evenings.

Concerts on winter Sunday evenings were one of the best meeting places for the village community. Everyone took part in them. The concert itself would occupy the first part of the evening, then all the chairs would be moved and dancing would take place. The night would end merrily with the strain of the music heard in the village until quite far into the night. We had never been allowed to stay to the end of any of the concert-dances. I cannot say that for myself I minded about this, for by half-past ten I felt tired and ready to go home. I liked my bedtime more at times than I liked the dancing. My elder sister, of course, made loud protests at having to come home just when the fun really started. This not without reason because her friends were allowed out later than she was and naturally this was very upsetting for her.

Papa was very strict. Concert yes, but one must be home by half-past ten. A few times we arrived home nearer to eleven than to the stated time and the trouble it caused wasn't worth the extra half an hour's fun. Jean wasn't very keen on those concert nights for it was him who had the task of seeing his sisters home at the stated hour. He used to get quite upset having to constantly remind his sisters that it was time to go home. I have known boyfriends of my sister trying to buy him off by providing him with lemonade and sweets. Jean would settle down for a few minutes – in fact, just long enough for him to eat and drink what was provided – then, "Come on, let's go home," would once again be heard.

The day following the concert our friends would amble to our home to tell us what we had missed by leaving the concert early. They behaved as if leaving early was something we did from choice. "Surely you can ask your father to stay a bit later," were their usual comments. Papa was a bit of a charmer where ladies and girls were concerned and it was very hard for our friends to believe that the same man who welcomed them full of smiles was the stern father we had to live with . . . Our "Oh, but Papa is very severe," would fall on totally deaf ears, as our friends would fall over themselves to be nice to Papa if he walked in the room. I could never understand this, surely it would have been better for us if they had ignored him, he might have wondered a bit about his unpopularity then. At times I used to feel our friends were traitors to us with their niceties to our too vigilant – or so we felt – father.

Still, despite the early 'curfew' we had lovely times. To young eyes life can be really magical. I would watch the loving couples dancing tightly embraced on the dance floor and feel it was so nice to see this open display of feelings. My turn would come, some day I would be the object of someone's admiration, someone's love; of this I never doubted.

What I liked best was taking part in plays. I loved the dressing-up, the putting on of make-up, which I would leave on my face until I returned home. Maman would exclaim, "Have we got a clown in the house?" She was joking, of course, she too had a lot of fun listening to us recounting all the ups and downs of life as an 'artiste'. One had to be so versatile in a village where the number of players were limited. I was in turn a gypsy, a butcher's boy, a blind girl, a Spanish senorita; and that is to name just a few of the roles I clearly remember playing.

Sometimes some of the elders put on shows called 'Revues', all about current affairs – very well staged, these were. The songs for the show were written by the local people and they were very catchy numbers. Andrimont was such a happy place for us in those days, we were growing up in a very pleasant and very relaxed manner. At our home there was no opportunity for loneliness and in our village no room for boredom. What more can children want at the start of their journey through life.

Our village naturally had some outstanding personalities and none was quite as outstanding as the village priest – Monsieur le Curé Sevrin. He was a tall spare figure, a man who the day he took over the parish adopted the villagers as his children. He loved them, served them and cared for them with utmost devotion. On matters of religion he was a strict disciplinarian. He expected one and all to walk always on the straight and narrow path, or so it seemed from listening to the admonitions which he gave from the pulpit of the church in a very forceful fashion. However, he had a heart of gold, and although he could be very strict, an erring member of his community would only find kindness on returning to the fold.

The children of the village were both in awe of him and loved him dearly. To them he was God's law not to be ignored and to them he was God's mercy and love, a balm for one's misdeeds.

To my family Monsieur le Curé was always very kind. The fact that he was the priest who was in charge of the church, the teaching of religion to the children and the pointer of God's way for his parishioners, did not make him remote from the problems of the day to day life of a large family. He was aware that a large family's financial standing was as important as its religious attitude and that, in fact, keeping an eye on one meant keeping an eye on the other.

There were other large families in the village. They too received support as we did. When Papa had problems during his house rebuilding period, our kind priest had offered to send workers to help Papa. The offer wasn't accepted but this was only because our father had such definite views as to how he wanted the work done and he preferred to work alone.

The life of a village is full of happenings. In fact, it could almost be said that a village's life might as well be lived in the open, for everything came under scrutiny. Life and death were facets of the village's life which affected everyone; the latest baby, the latest deceased, were either welcomed or mourned as was appropriate and everyone took part, but no one as much as Monsieur le Curé, he was always on the spot almost immediately. The church and the presbytery dominated the village but the domination was one of benevolence and real deep-felt pastoral care.

The sisters at the Convent took second place in the personalities stake after the priest, at least so far as I was concerned. I was educated by them. The nuns were ladies devoted to the task of educating the village children; boys and girls to the age of six then girls to the age of fourteen. The Convent also took in boarding pupils. When we were going to the Convent there were always at least ten girls boarding, these girls were mostly farmer's daughters whose home was a bit too far away to make the journey daily. The Convent was a lovely house, to me it was the holy of holies. It was clean and the floors shone – so much so that if for some reason I was sent to the house, I felt like walking on my head. Not that this was necessary because the nuns who were responsible for the highly polished floors had rugs distributed at strategic points so one would not step onto the floors. Sometimes a group of girls would go over to the house to help with the polishing. The polishing was done by putting on polishing 'shoes'; small padded mats which fitted over your own shoes, it was like being on a skating rink, we loved it. When volunteers were requested for this task I would be amongst the first to put up my hand.

Sister Celine was our favourite nun. She was an elderly nun who took charge of the infant class. The word infant could mean a baby at that time; mostly though the children were from two and a half years old, when they were termed 'dry'. Sister Celine kept a supply of childish underwear for those who had, alas, waited too long. Our dear little sister would simply change the child's underwear and rinse the garment without a second thought.

To the nuns, Monsieur le Curé was a very important person whose word was law. He was the school religious supervisor. The Convent's head being Mère Supérieure. A visit to the school from Monsieur le Curé was regarded as an occasion. From our classroom we could see the large porch door which led into the school-yard. If Monsieur le Curé walked through the door, hands in the classroom would go up immediately to announce, "Here is Monsieur le Curé, Sister."

Sister would look around the class as if to reassure herself that we were presentable. She would remind us to look industrious and not to forget to stand up when Monsieur le Curé walked into the classroom, then she would fold her arms across her chest, her hands pushed inside her sleeves, and we would await the arrival of the priest. Soon, in the company of Mère Supérieure, Monsieur le Curé would enter the classroom. We children would be working furiously to give a good impression of our application where our schoolwork was concerned. Then as one we would stand up with a resonant, "Bonjour Monsieur le Curé." Sister would smile, pleased with her class and its good behaviour.

Monsieur le Curé always brought sweets for the children, but Mère Supérieure, to whom the sweets were handed for distribution, was a hoarder. Into her sweet box went the latest treat, to be handed to us when she felt we deserved it, and we knew that it would be a long time before that day came. Some Easter eggs once tasted of mould before they were finally awarded, and as quickly as the children's thanks were said the chocolate was spat out and disposed of in one's handkerchief surreptitiously.

It was at the season of Santa Claus that Monsieur le Curé excelled himself. He really came into his own then. A concert was arranged by the nuns and the teacher of the boys school. Plays were performed, choirs sang and monologues were rendered, all with great enthusiasm. Then Santa Claus would arrive. The elder children trying very hard to guess who was behind the beard and the wig, while the younger children clung tight to their parents hands, just in case . . .

Then came the great moment of the evening, the moment when the children collected their parcelled-up gifts. The contents of the parcels owed a lot to Monsieur le Curé's efforts on the children's behalf, both in the way of donations sought from industries and shops and all the efforts for fund-raising events undertaken with the unfailing support of our beloved priest.

Once a year the school trip took place. When I was at school this was the most exciting occasion of the year. As children we seldom travelled. We had an Aunt and Uncle who lived in Battice, which wasn't all that far but the easiest way to get there was by train. I had travelled there a few times with Maman and I loved the train journeys, to me there wasn't a mode of transport which gave me as much pleasure. But unfortunately train journeys were seldom undertaken and when Maman's sister and family had moved to Brussels, this put an end to any chances of visiting them. But we had the yearly school trip to look forward to, and I waited patiently all the year for that occasion.

Of course I wasn't the only one. At my home all those who were old enough to go talked of nothing else once the school trip had been arranged. We would make preparations as if we were going on a world cruise rather than a trip around the local beauty spots. Maman, who could see how excited we were, was full of 'dos and don'ts'. Actually she need not have worried for we had a great sense of responsibility towards each other and were always very aware of what the other members of our family were doing.

The school trips were responsible for our knowledge of the beauty of the countryside all around the part of Belgium where we lived. We once visited Luxembourg; this is perhaps the nicest trip I remember because it gave me a chance to see another country. One day we all hoped that we would have the opportunity to visit the country of our father, England. It would be a long time before this happened, I felt, for a lot of money was needed to go there.

Chapter Twenty

'Houch of a Thousand Gods' was one of our village's most colourful characters. 'Houch' who was reputed to have been, at some time in his life, a professor, was now a rustic. He wore a long, grey smock as peasants did in olden days, his feet were shod in clogs, his long hair flowing around his head. His shuffling walk aided by a wooden stick, he went in and around the village swearing under his breath as he passed, "Thousand gods, thousand gods," hence the name by which he was known to us. He passed on his way, totally unaware of anyone around him.

We were frightened of him, so to be on the right side of him we gave him a polite "Bonjour monsieur" which he ignored. Yet it would not be true to say that he disliked children. He left everyone alone and went on his way. It was probably the mystery of the old man which gave him awesome qualities. He was seen each day, at about the same time, coming up the hill and going past our house on his way back to the village. "Here's Houch!" someone would shout and we would wait until he had passed before we returned to our games. He lived alone in a tiny house in the village centre. Sometimes we would try to peep through the tiny windows, jumping to catch a quick glimpse of the interior, for the windows were rather high off the ground. The interior told us exactly nothing about 'Houch'. At some time in our youth 'Houch' disappeared from the village scene. We did not ask what had become of him, nor did we hear mention of him. Probably the old man went to live in a home for his last days.

There were other intriguing things to occupy us and fire our imagination. On the way to the village from Sous-le-Chateau was a very large house. It was fully furnished but no one appeared to live there permanently. The house was almost totally out of sight from the road, with high hedges and a porch-like gate at the front. One side, however, was accessible. On that side was a large bay window facing the road. We used to stand on anything we could find to look inside the room, for on one wall was a large fearful picture of the devil. As we passed to and fro on our way to the village, we never failed to have a look at the devil. We were frightened of the picture but still we sought to catch a glimpse of it, then ran home as fast as we could to get away from the fearful face with the malevolent looks and the awesome horns.

When we were older we learned that a family from Brussels owned the house as a holiday place. As for the fearful picture, it was simply a painting of Mephistopheles, a fictional character from an opera. A member of the family had once taken the part in a production of the opera. The truth wasn't as exciting as our imagined interpretations.

Andrimont, like everywhere, had its share of elderly people, some of whom lived alone. As I have already said, we made those the recipients of our good deeds. There is a good deed that I remember well as it spoiled what I had hoped was going to be a very good evening for me.

Mrs Loxaine was a very stout old lady who lived in a house at the entrance to the village. She spent much of her time looking out of the window from the upstairs small flat where she lived. Sometimes we did messages for her. She would lower the money in a paper bag tied at the end of a string and when we had made the acquisition of her requirements we too would tie the goods to the string to be taken up by her.

One evening Madeleine and I were on our way to a concert at the Cercle la Concorde. We had on our best Sunday clothes and Maman had permitted us to stay to watch the dancing which always took place after the concert was over.

I had perfumed myself with Therese's perfume just in case I was asked for a dance; after all I was fifteen now and fancy-free. We came abreast of Madame Loxaine's house on our way to the concert and she was at her upstairs window as usual. As we went past she called, "Is that the little Docherty girls?"

"Yes Madame," we replied.

"Could you come and light my lamp dears, I will drop you the key," she said. She explained that a lady from the village came every day to light her lamp. She had not come that day and the old lady could not trust herself to light the lamp. I could not trust myself either but I could not refuse to help the old lady. We asked for the key to be lowered and after retrieving it, we went inside to see what I could do. The lamp had to be refilled and this was a messy job. I did my best and after a while success was mine, the lamp was lit. Madame Loxaine was all thanks, she wished us a lovely time at the concert-dance.

We were not out of the house two minutes when I realised that I was well and truly perfumed. Alas, it wasn't Therese's perfume that I could smell anymore, it was paraffin! My coat smelled, my dress and my hands smelled.

"Wave them about," advised Madeleine.

I danced about shaking my clothes and waving my arms in the air. I wished that I was still a little girl and washed my hands in rain puddles as I had done in years past. My whole evening was ruined. At the concert hall I hid myself at the back, fearing to be known by the village boys as 'Paraffin Marguerite', they could be so cruel at times like these.

Later on, when we returned home, I complained bitterly to Maman about my predicament. I almost said that it was her fault when I remarked, "That's what happens when parents insist that their children do good work!"

"The next time something like that happens again go to Aunt Miou, she will help," concluded Maman. I wished that I had thought of that!

Other members of my family thought of Aunt Miou's house as a possible place of help. Her outside toilet was a very good stop for those of us who were overcome by a sense of urgency.

One of my younger brothers one day was so overcome that he created a state of emergency when he arrived home crying, "I have had an accident in the toilet."

"Oh dear . . ." said Maman who was busy making a meal. "Can you see to it?" she turned to me.

I did not like the idea but needs must! I went to examine our 'loo'. Returning to the living-room I said, "It's all right."

My young brother cried even harder, if that was possible.

"Oh dear," said Maman when my brother announced that it wasn't our toilet he was referring to, "whose toilet is it then?" she asked.

"Aunt Miou's," he sobbed.

"Oh dear," said Maman, this time with consternation.

My brother's face suddenly brightened. "I didn't tell, they will not know it's me," he concluded.

"It must be cleaned," declared Maman.

Oh dear! thought I. And just as I thought Maman looked at me, "I'll go," I said at once, feeling the sooner this sad episode was over the better. I gathered a pail of warm water, a scrubbing brush, a cloth and some soap. My young brother came along to carry the needed cleaning gear and we set off for the village.

I must say that I was glad to get inside the toilet and get on with my job. So I scrubbed inside the toilet while my brother kept a watch outside to warn would-be users of its temporary 'out-of-use' state.

Our Aunt, hearing the strange noises coming from the garden, came to investigate. She found me inside the toilet scrubbing for all I was worth. "What are you doing?" she asked.

I explained the unfortunate incident and how I had been sent to put things right. She shook her head, "All you had to do was tell me. My goodness, it's not such a terrible thing." Now that the job was done I agreed with her. With my young brother now all smiles I returned home carrying the pail – in my home life was full of happenings, one never knew what one might be called to do next.

At times I had wished that I was an only child then I had second thoughts, that day I really wished that I was an only child!

Chapter Twenty-one

It was the fateful year of 1939. I had worked in town for one year and was thoroughly enjoying it. I liked the shop where I was employed. It was situated at the corner of the main square in the town. I liked Verviers which was then a very busy town full of life, and in the shop I was consequently very busy attending to the needs of the many customers.

Having come to terms with the fact that I would never be a famous singer, I settled for the simple things of life, hoping that perhaps one day I might marry a rich man. This I regarded as a distinct possibility. The shop where I worked had some very wealthy customers and it was me who was given the job of taking the monthly bills round to their homes. I caught glimpses of the lovely interiors of the homes where they lived. Once or twice, on the occasion when a prompt settlement of the bill had been made, I was shown by a butler or a maid into a little side room. My young head, filled with the romantic encounters of the screen's lovers, saw, one day, something similar happening to me, I could see myself with my whole family, whom I would not leave behind, moving into one of those wealthy homes with me as the new mistress.

Maman had not been in very good health for a while. She decided that she could do with some help at home. It was with regret that I gave my notice at the shop and the ladies for whom I worked were sad at losing me for I was a good worker and could be trusted with any tasks given. Maman's needs came first, however, and back at home I took charge of my share of household work, showing the same thoroughness that I had shown at my work.

When I had time on my hands, I read and I visited the

neighbours. I became a real little gossip. Maman, who never had much time for anything else but her family problems, found herself being told the life stories of the people in our direct neighbourhood. Personally I was fascinated that so much we knew nothing about had gone on in the village. I had always felt that knowing everyone was enough, now I knew *about* everyone and my eyes were opening to facets of life I had been totally unaware existed. However, after a while Maman discouraged my frequent visits, I probably brought home stories which my mother felt I was rather young to be told. Instead I joined the church choir and went to rehearsals twice a week. There were gossips there as well, so now I had two very enjoyable occupations in singing and gossiping and it relieved the monotony of the housework chores.

Maman's friend Mariette had resigned her job as governess to the children of the castle. In fact, she had become redundant as the three young girls were now attending a school in town. Soon afterwards she was married to a man who had been regarded in the village as a confirmed bachelor, thus proving there is no such an individual once the right person comes along. Mariette became pregnant and she found in Maman a good confidante for all the problems that beset her. She was often at our home where she was welcomed with a good cup of coffee – Maman's speciality.

One day she came to bring bad news; the baby she was carrying was dead inside her. Mariette was broken-hearted, it was possibly the only chance she would ever have of having a child of her own. It did not seem fair, she had cared for others' children and now she would be denied her own child.

Mariette lived in the caretaker's house alongside the porch at the entrance to the Chateau's garden, this was directly in front of our house. One day my eyes did not leave her bedroom window; doctors were with her as she gave birth to a still-born child. We were very upset for her.

When I try to remember the early part of 1939, all I can remember are talks of troops massing along the frontier as if the German army was planning an attack on Belgium. Therese had a new boyfriend and his father had a car which he allowed his son to use at weekends. I would join my sister and her boyfriend on 'randonnées'; we would go as near to the frontier as we dared, to see if there were any truths in the reports. We saw a few uniformed men and barbed wire but there was no army in sight. We were reassured. Spring gave way to summer and we were still at peace, and thankful for it.

In July the village fair appeared as usual and in our home Grand-mère came to stay. Grand-mère, who we all called Marraine, meaning godmother, was the most travelled member of our family. In our early years we had shared a house with her and Grand-père. They lived on the first storey of the house, while we lived on the second storey. When Grand-père reached retirement age he passed his printing business on to his sons and with Marraine they lived what I regarded to be a very exciting life. They were always either getting on or getting off a train.

They had brought nine children into the world, had educated them and had run a printing business. When their family were all settled, either to rear their own families or to go into religious life, as two of our uncles had done – one serving God in caring for Indian children, the other a Christian brother teaching at a large college in Luxembourg – our grandparents enjoyed their later years travelling around from one family to the other.

One sad day, on arrival in Verviers after one of those trips, Grand-père had collapsed at the railway station and died suddenly. I was still quite young at the time of the passing of Grand-père. All I remembered of the funeral which was a very well attended event, for Grand-père had been a very prominent citizen of the town, were many tearful aunts and uncles. Maman had been dressed entirely in black, a veil covering her face. She took Therese and I into Uncle Paul's study where, on a black covered stand, lay a large coffin with tall lit candles around it. In the face of something we only dimly understood, we had stood, two little girls with their mourning mother, as a last good-bye to Grand-père.

Marraine was alone and, if it was possible, she travelled even more than before. We visited her when she was in 'residence' at Uncle Paul's house. Despite her busy life she always had time for her grandchildren. We were very fond of her.

Our family being so large we had not been able to have Marraine staying at our home, as much as we would have loved to have her living with us for a while.

In the summer of 1939, Maman, her last child well on its feet, the nappies put away for good and with daughters old enough to help when needed and sons as well, for we all had tasks to perform, invited her mother to spend a holiday at our home. Marraine chose the time of the fair for her visit. She was born in Andrimont and in her youth had greatly enjoyed the time of the fair. It would be a lovely trip down memory lane for her.

The news that Marraine was to stay at our home was received with joy by all. We loved her very dearly. We three girls cleaned the house even more thoroughly than usual. Therese polished all Maman's brass ornaments until they shone and we could see our faces in them. Fresh net curtains were put in every window. Our home had a real festive air for the arrival of our dear Marraine.

A taxi brought her to the gate one Saturday and Marraine settled herself in our home. She was happy to be there, and she sang gay little songs for Anne, Pierre and Fernand, who stood at her side. Then she sat in the garden under the greengage trees, and there on the large table we ate our lunch. Marraine talked of years gone by, of Maman's youth and escapades.

The fair's opening was at two o'clock and we all walked to the village to spend the afternoon in a happy and carefree atmosphere, with the roundabout turning merrily and the swings balanced in the air in a 'couldn't care less' manner. At the tombola stall Fernand won a prize that he immediately presented to Marraine. We returned home at tea-time to eat our festive tea under the trees.

In her youth Marraine had loved dancing, so when evening fell Papa offered to look after the younger children so that Maman could accompany Marraine who had decided she was going to the evening fun.

Therese, as usual, danced every dance and I had a few admirers myself. Jean was at the shooting gallery reducing clay pipes to pieces with David and Rene as audience; because this year they were counting carefully, I doubted their big brother would claim the fantastic results he had done in the past when no one stood by.

With the other children in bed under Papa's care, Maman looked very happy watching the dancing with Marraine. It was a really lovely evening with the villagers, as usual, making the most of the yearly rejoicing. The dancing was getting livelier as the hours passed by.

A policeman from the small town of Dison appeared on 'Le

Place' and someone pointed Maman and our group out to him. I felt suddenly very apprehensive, something was wrong, terribly wrong. He beckoned Maman to go over to him. We all waited, frightened of the unusual situation. Marraine had seen in our faces the signs of fear, she held Madeleine's and my hands in hers. Maman returned to our group.

"We have to go home," she said, "the policeman is going to escort us." That was all she said at first.

"Why Maman?" I asked. "Why?"

"We are in danger. Go and get Therese off the dance floor and tell her we are going home." Then she sent Madeleine for the boys at the shooting gallery.

When we were all together, we were all asking questions:

"What is the matter?"

"What's happened?" David asked. "Is our house on fire?"

"There is trouble at the first cottage, and the policeman wants to see us safely home. Mr Wronsky is very drunk and savage with it," said Maman.

Wronsky, as we called him, was a man that nearly all of us feared. He was a German Pole married to a German woman. Since he had come to live in the first cottage, he had caused much trouble to all the neighbours and to us more than anyone else. He professed to hate what he called "British mad people".

He was a huge man with a massive face, brutish looking, always scowling, and he disliked children intensely. To us he was what we regarded as the typical hun, a man to keep well away from, a man to fear. Once he had threatened one of my brothers with an axe, which probably his idea of fun, but the boy was so frightened that it took days to get him to go to school. Maman had made a formal complaint about him and he was cautioned. After this he was even more unpleasant to all of us. His wife by contrast was a nice person, but only when we were assured that her monster of a husband was nowhere near would we stop to speak to her. They had two children but he kept them busy so they did not play very much.

Maman said Wronsky was creating trouble, but why the escort for us? We soon had the answer to that when the policeman said he wanted us all to go into our home unseen by Wronsky, if this was possible. Wronsky had made threats against us, as well as having terrorised his wife and children who were taking refuge in the attic above the cottage.

We listened to all that was said, very concerned but not quite as upset as our dear Marraine. What a regrettable thing to happen while she was staying at our home. She still held tight on to Madeleine's and my hands as we walked home.

Maman came over and took her mother's arm. "Don't be frightened, we will soon be indoors," said Maman.

"I hope so," said Marraine shaking her head.

Jean said to Maman, "If I make a hole in the hedge we could all get in by the side of the garden and not be seen."

The policeman agreed with Jean's idea.

As we neared our home we could see policemen and neighbours all milling around the road, then someone shouted, "Don't jump!"

We saw nothing else as we were told by the policeman to get into our home as quickly and as quietly as possible. Jean made a hole in the hedge and we helped Marraine, who was nearly eighty, and Maman into the garden. Then we all ran for the door and heaved a sigh of relief when it closed on us. Papa, who had requested the police escort for us, was glad that we were safely home.

That night there was little sleep for some of the members of our household. The drama at the cottage was concluded when firemen came from the town to rescue the stranded family. Then the family was driven away with a police escort. Meanwhile Wronsky, probably overcome by liquor, had gone indoors after waving his axe menacingly at all those present.

Maman, Marraine, Therese and I could not sleep. We looked out of the upstairs windows. Under the trees of the small park in front of our house, we could see the red glow of the cigarettes in the mouths of the policemen who kept a vigil throughout the night.

When daylight came we were feeling more relaxed and went to bed. The following day our dear Marraine packed all her things. "Renee, I could not stay another day," she explained. We understood for it had been a nasty experience for us too. When we saw her to the waiting taxi I felt very angry with the brutal man who was the cause of Marraine's departure after such a short stay.

Wronsky was expelled from the village by the authorities soon afterwards and we heaved a sigh of relief. If all Germans were like Wronsky I felt that I was right in fearing them.

One day, while doing some shopping in town for my mother, I nearly collided with him. He did not recognise me. I hoped he never would, for I found it hard to forget that he had said he would kill us all if the war ever came.

Chapter Twenty-two

The 3rd of September 1939 was a day that I will always remember. On this fateful day I saw Papa cry for the first time in my life. He sat on a chair, a large handkerchief held to his face . . . and sobbed.

Grouped around him, we watched our father, the confident Englishman, cry for his country which had just entered into war with Germany.

To me, at the time, war had seemed inevitable. Hitler and his monstrous gang had not re-armed Germany for nothing. We had followed through the radio and the newspapers, the efforts of Mr Chamberlain, the peace-maker, during the negotiations that preceded the opening of the hostilities. To me Hitler was a very cunning person. I had made my own conclusions, they were not optimistic, quite the reverse in fact.

Maman had been reassuring. Her argument being that after the heavy loss of life which had occurred during the 1914-18 war on Belgian soil, our country would be regarded as a place well left alone. Uncle Paul wasn't so optimistic: "Take the children to England, sell the house," were his advocations. He would shake his head, looking very sad. "You are not safe here," he would say. More than this he could not tell. Being a member of the Intelligence Service he was well informed. It must have been very hard for him not to tell us firmly that there were very good indications of the war being imminent. All he could do was look at us sadly.

So finally, as Uncle Paul had tried to tell us many times, war had been declared between England and Germany. Papa was heart-broken and we were fearful. Later on that day a telegram was delivered to our home. It was an urgent message from the

British Consulate in Liège – 'Consider your family unsafe advise your return to England' – it said.

There was consternation in our home. We must leave everything we had known up to now for something so totally different as life in England must be.

Papa had always assured us that life in England was wonderful. Sometimes we talked amongst ourselves of the hope that someday we would visit that country. Many a night I had lain in bed make-believing that I was actually on a train going to England. Sometimes, standing beside the rail of the pond near our home, I had forgotten my surroundings and looking at the water only, imagined myself on a ship on my way to the country of my father. But my 'dream' trips were only of holidays spent there . . . now we must go there to live!

Papa and Maman discussed far into the night how to take their family to safety. The next day Papa wrote to the Consulate asking for financial assistance and he also wrote to his family in England for help in finding some accommodation.

The Consul's reply came back by the next post and it said simply – 'I regret that financial help is not available' – just that.

From Papa's family the message was – 'Will do all we can to help'.

The only possible source of money for us was the house. A large board was put prominently announcing that the house was for sale. My feelings were very mixed at the time. The war was a frightening prospect, but travelling was alluring. Sometimes my mind would dwell on thoughts of the horrors of one and other times I was rather excited that we probably would very soon leave for England. I had long discussions with my two sisters as to where life would lead us now.

Therese was firmly against going to England; she was in love with a Belgian boy so her heart was in Belgium. If she had to leave it would be heart-breaking for her. To the rest of the family going to England was like a welcome adventure; there was a proviso though, we would wish to return to Belgium eventually. None of us envisaged leaving that country, which we regarded as home, for good. We all loved our life in Belgium where we had always been very happy. As we were young the call of adventure was alluring, so going to England for a while wasn't daunting. Selling the house was, but Maman said that this was unavoidable and we would buy a home in town when we came back.

During this strange situation Maman said very little. She watched Papa's efforts to take the family out of possible danger and she got on with the day to day task of caring for her family.

To all our friends the large placard on the house announcing its sale said it all. They came to visit us now more than they ever had, and they were sad that soon we might leave them.

The weeks and the months passed. No offers were made for the house. It was a time when the world waited and watched the clouds gathering. There was a war yet there was no war.

One day Uncle Paul told Maman that the Germans would invade Belgium in the spring. Maman said nothing to us about it.

We noticed that the fortress of Battice which we could see from our bedroom windows showed signs of activities. Manoeuvres were taking place fairly often. This wasn't the only sign that all was not well. In the spring many men were conscripted. Amongst them was Mariette's husband and Monsieur Ducas, the owner of the Chateau. Madame Ducas and her three daughters left for Brussels by car one day and the Chateau was closed. Little by little the clouds of war were gathering over our little village. The men we had known as the village's tradesmen and farmers, now walked in the village, while on leave, wearing uniforms.

Winter passed, then the snow melted away. The primroses, the violets, the buttercups and the daffodils were in bloom once again, the weather was mild and it was a beautiful spring. March and April passed. Once again there were alarming reports of German troops massing along the frontier.

Then we were in May. There were still no offers for our home. I painted all the outside doors and windows, and the gate, to make our home more attractive to prospective buyers.

Spring would soon give way to summer, the weather was absolutely marvellous, the war was beginning to seem remote. During the beautiful days the threatening clouds did not seem quite so menacing any more. There were rumours that Hitler was dying of cancer, rumours of rifts in the German army; would they turn on their leaders rather than march into other countries? We were somehow comforted by all those rumours, especially those about the days of reckoning for Hitler.

I was only young but, like all those I knew, I hated that

monster. He stood for all that we never wanted to see happen: war, devastation, ruin and fear. If he was dying of cancer, soon his leadership would end and very likely peace would be signed between England and Germany. There would be no war to fight.

It was amazing how rumours travelled – 'demoralisation' and 'fifth columnist' were words that we had not yet heard mentioned.

Life in the village was going on almost as usual despite the rumours and the counter rumours of troops massing along the frontier. Then one of our neighbours fell asleep on a train and unwittingly passed into Germany. She was detained there for a while; the poor lady had great difficulty convincing the German authorities that she wasn't a spy, that her arrival into their country was an unfortunate mistake. Finally she was taken back to the frontier under escort and handed over to the Belgian police. The lady was a good friend of Maman and that incident had quite an effect on me, and the thought of the distress that the lady suffered remained on my mind for a long time.

Sometimes we had driven with a friend to the frontier on Sundays but now we avoided going near the border with Germany. It would be so dangerous for Therese and I who were English. This thought had occurred to Maman as well, in fact she was so worried that we gave up going for drives altogether.

Strangely enough, despite the feeling that the world was watching and waiting for Hitler's next move, and Belgium was a prime target, in our youth we tried very hard to be optimistic. Spring was here, all was new again, and surely the worst never happens. The pleasant world we knew would not crumble, it couldn't, it mustn't . . .

As the months passed the house remained unsold and we found no way of raising the money, so all plans for going to England were abandoned. When plans were made in case of invasion Maman, with Madame Fadier and Mariette, agreed that the belt of fortresses built along and around the River Meuse should keep the invaders in check. If we went behind the River Meuse we could wait there until the invaders had been defeated. It seemed at the time a safe measure and gave us a certain degree of security, but we hoped that moving away from our home would never prove to be necessary.

That year it was my brother Rene who was making his Solemn Communion. It was such a lovely spring and our garden was beautiful. Maman's flower garden was in bloom, giving a colourful display. As I was at home to help I was looking around for ways to brighten up our home. I cleaned the house from top to bottom, for we were having a party to celebrate Rene's Communion.

Maman went to town with my brother to buy all the clothes necessary to make him very smart for that important day. The armband worn by the boy communicants, a white and gold-embroidered knot finished with a fringe, lay in its box in a drawer in Maman's room. It had already been worn twice, once by Jean and once by David on the day of their Communion.

The presents for my brother were arriving and from his godfather he received a watch. We all thought him really lucky to get such a lovely gift.

The first Sunday in May was a lovely sunny day, it was the day of the Solemn Communion. The ritual of the day, the wonderful church services, the bride-like small girls and the smartly dressed young boys, all went on as usual.

I cannot remember anything that might have overshadowed that day. Uncle Paul and Aunt Jose, Maman's brother-in-law, our Uncle Emile and our two cousins Madeleine and Emile, Great Aunt Madeleine, who had recently come to live near us, all came to join us for the afternoon tea.

Most of the day was spent in the garden and walking around. Madeleine and I took Aunt Jose and Great Aunt Madeleine to the village and around the small paths through the fields to admire the countryside in its yearly display of spring flowers.

We ate a lovely meal later on that day. Uncle Paul did not forget his tour of the garden and made his usual small jokes about Papa's 'fortifications' and his 'Maginot line'.

In the evening we had a fireworks display. Some of our young friends came to join us and it was a very happy group that watched the 'shooting stars', the 'catherine wheels' and the very impressive 'Roman candles' light up the darkness of the night sky.

Later on there were the good-byes and kisses, as our relatives took their leave. Then the party was over. Yet another member of our family had been a Communicant. Happy, we all went to bed, putting away our best Sunday clothes for another week, or so we thought . . .

It was on the Friday morning that the explosions woke us . . . many of those we had said good-bye to we were never to see again.

That first war morning we gave little thought to anyone, we were in such danger. There was only one thing for us to do, so when Papa finally said, "Quick everyone, get ready, we are leaving . . ." there was very little hesitation.

Without a backward glance we left our home and all we had known up to then. Our home had become somewhere to run away from . . . our village a place to leave behind, without even a single good-bye to those who had peopled our lives. Our friends, our relations, all those dear to us, in a moment all this was part of the past, as we ran . . .

Chapter Twenty-three

Papa stood up and shouted, "Quick everyone, get ready, we are leaving."

All that morning we had waited for that moment, but when it finally came we were in such a desperate situation, with the Germans nearing the village, that panic seized us all.

Maman was trying desperately to keep some order by giving each one of us a specific task. I was to fill the food hamper with any type of food that could be carried. Fear made me tearful, and trembling I tried my best to do as Maman had told me. Therese had to fill a suitcase with some clothes from the linen cupboard. She too was visibly shaking as she threw bundles of clothes taken at random from the shelves. Jean was getting coats from the coat cupboard, he had decided that his new bike wasn't going to be left behind. "It will be useful," agreed Maman as she helped him balance the coats over the handlebars. Madeleine, with David and Paul, had brought the blanket packs downstairs and we slung the five packs over our shoulders.

Papa had dressed Pierre and they were already outside the house waiting with impatience for departure. Little Anne, who did not understand anything else but the fact that we were going out somewhere, was running about excitedly. A coldness had come over me; I felt like a robot, my tears had dried on my face. I kept looking at Maman's face, desperately wanting her to say something comforting. In those desperate moments all she could do was to hurry us.

Soon we were all out of the house, down the path and out of the garden gate. We left our home without even a backward glance. We walked past the cottages then made our way through the small lane which took us on the road to Verviers.

Andrimont was left behind and I felt no pangs of regret . . . just fear, blind naked fear. As we got on the road to Verviers there was no one in sight. Quickly we made our way downhill. In about twenty minutes, filled with apprehension lest we were overtaken by the advancing enemy, we entered the town.

Papa said, "We must go to the railway station, perhaps there will be a train for Brussels. Once there we could go to the Consulate where we should be helped."

We had hurried all the way from Andrimont and already Pierre and Little Anne were slowing us down. Poor little children, because we were all so worried they were beginning to realise this was no ordinary outing. Pierre kept asking anxiously, "Will the Germans hurt us Papa?" Fernand and Paul held hands and although saying nothing they looked very frightened.

We were passing the police station and Papa decided to go in to ask if help for foreign families was available. Soon he came out shaking his head. "There's no help available," he reported, then added, "and there is no use our going to the railway station either, there are no trains leaving anymore. We must walk to Liège, that's our only possibility of escape."

This was really shocking – no trains! And we must walk to Liège . . . We will never make it I felt, the Germans will get there before us. They had tanks, army vehicles and cars, how could we hope to escape?

Maman had a hopeless look on her face. I felt that her thoughts were very much like mine. She made no remarks at first. Maman, always so courageous, the firm rock in our family, banishing all our fears and worries, at that moment could only see us standing around her worried and panicky. Finally she took a deep breath then she spoke, "Come on, if walk we must, let's get started." Somehow she managed to make those few words sound almost optimistic.

"Come on," we all said, "let's get started."

The town of Verviers was almost deserted. We walked through it with as much haste as we could muster considering the small children which the elder ones almost dragged along. When Verviers was left behind our parents decided that we would keep off the main roads, it would be better if we made our way to Liège through the country. The German army was likely to stay on the main roads on its march of conquest. If we kept to the country roads we might escape somehow; we must try every way possible to avoid meeting them.

We climbed slowly upwards on our way to the country. There were other refugees like ourselves who had decided on the same route. We walked in the afternoon sunshine, slowly putting a few more kilometres between us and the invaders.

Papa had worked out that the Germans would first take the town of Verviers and settle themselves there before pressing on to Liège. Papa, of course, was making his assumptions on how the German army would proceed with the invasion, with his know-how of tactics from the 1914-18 war. Maman wasn't too sure that he was correct. After all, what we knew of the German army through propaganda was not reassuring. The Germans had a very modern and powerful army. They made inroads quickly in the countries they invaded. However, Maman discouraged any talk of what might or might not happen; it was best to put all one's efforts into getting away as far and as fast as one could in her view.

During the summer we often went for walks with Maman, sometimes we would walk for an hour and more, but we certainly had never done the kind of walking which was needed today – walking on and on – making the shortest possible stops to seek water to drink or to have some rest. If one of us had a stone in his or her shoe and sat on the side of the road to remove it, all would sit by the roadside until the offending stone was removed. There were moans of "I don't feel like walking any more" or "My feet hurt", and Maman would say, "The Germans are behind us, remember." This caused the sitters to stand up and once again take wearily to the road.

Passing some houses I saw a lady lying on the ground lifeless. I looked in alarm, "Oh Maman has she been shot?" I queried almost in tears.

"She probably fainted. Don't look, you can't help her," said Maman quickly.

There were people around the lady, it was obvious that she would be helped and Maman was right, it was best not to look. I had been very upset by the sight of this poor lady lying alongside the pavement, for it had dawned on me that we might see people who had been killed. They would look like that; lifeless, pitiful, like broken dolls, and it might even be one of us! Quickly I

Koningin Emma

The Dutch cross channel steamer which the Docherty family of twelve just managed to catch with the help of two soldiers. It left Bayonne, France on the evening tide of the 25th June 1940, arriving in Plymouth, England twenty-four hours later, after being pursued by an enemy submarine. They docked at Plymouth on the 26th June 1940, the day France fell to the German invasion.

The Docherty family arrive in England.
This photograph was taken on their arrival in England. It is taken from a newspaper cutting so is very poor quality, but is the only photograph with all twelve family members included:
Back: Jean, Marguerite, Marie-Therese, Renee-Marie (Maman) and David (Papa).
Front: Anne, Pierre, Fernand, Paul, Rene, Danny and Madeleine.

Danny, Peter, Anne, Rene, Fernand and Paul Docherty
at Hebburn Colliery, 1941.

David Docherty, 1952,
twelve years after his arrival back in England.

Marguerite, 29 years old.

Marguerite with her husband Joe.

chased the frightening thoughts out of my mind. I went over to Therese and offered to carry the hamper.

We stopped alongside a small wood to eat at tea-time. Maman shared bread and cheese amongst us then we ate some sugar lumps for stamina. There were no houses in sight so we must wait for something to drink. We did not enjoy our meal, in fact we made it only a hurried snack for we had become eager to go on. Soon we came to some houses, they were deserted and we went inside for water. A small bird in a cage attracted our attention. Madeleine took the cage outside and released the bird. It struck me forcibly then that we knew there would be no going home for some time for the people who lived there, as there wouldn't for us either. The small bird flew away in the afternoon sunshine.

Soon we were back on the road walking away from the houses. I wished that we had wings like the small bird. I was so afraid of the war machine which I regarded as completely ruthless; my childish war stories had frightened me, and now I was like the children of those stories running and hiding from the huns. My brothers and sisters spoke very little; it was as if we were all plagued with fearful thoughts which we did not want to share in case we spread more alarm than there was already.

Late that afternoon we came to a small town where most of the shops were closed. We entered a café and when Maman asked for refreshments the café owner shook her head and she looked really sad that she had nothing to offer us. She was leaving as soon as she had closed the shop. "We can't get away very far," she remarked, "we have to go to my mother, she is old and ill and she can't be moved; she will be so frightened." Everyone had troubles of some kind. We left the shop and went on our way. Little Anne and Pierre were crying, so Jean put Anne on top of the coats on his bicycle while Papa gave Pierre a lift by carrying him on his shoulders.

Maman was walking with a very thoughtful look on her face. I went up to her, "You look worried, will we not escape?" I asked. She looked at me and gave a sigh.

"I am thinking that we will have to look for somewhere to stay for the night, we can't go much further with everyone so tired, we must get some sleep."

"Where will we sleep?" I asked.

Maman shook her head. "I just don't know," she replied.

There was a group of people walking ahead of us. Papa went up to them. "What are you doing for the night?" he asked them.

"We will look for a large building – a school or somewhere like it – we will just have to sleep on the floor we guess," the man answered.

So we too set out to look for somewhere to sleep – a school preferably. First, of course, we must leave the country and find a town or even a village. Making for built-up areas we arrived at the small town of Prayon. It was dusk, the roads and the streets were deserted. We met again the group of people who were ahead of us earlier on. A man came over to us and he gave Papa directions to a school which he had been given himself. First we crossed over the railway lines, but soon we found ourselves back in the country again so we retraced our steps and we recrossed the railway lines. Will we never get there? I thought. Madeleine and Paul walked beside me and Paul had slipped his hand in mine. I held tight on to my young brother's hand – if I was frightened how must he feel?

We walked around the streets of the town looking for a large building, and suddenly we saw the school . . . it was like attaining salvation, we had a home for the night. The caretaker allowed us in and we distributed ourselves in one of the large schoolrooms. There were some tables. Our parents settled the two younger ones inside a reversed table. Then they laid two of our blankets on the floor, we took our coats off and rolled them to make pillows, then we lay on the blankets side by side.

Another family came into the classroom and there was some commotion until they too had settled.

Then three men walked into the room pushing the large door open with a loud bang. Some of us sat up, Maman pushed us down again. The Germans, I thought, oh my God, the Germans!

The men went and sat at a table and lit cigarettes, Maman whispered, "They are refugees like us."

We lay back very weary.

Suddenly through the skylight we saw a huge flash then heard the sound of gunfire; it was repeated again and again . . .

We fell asleep to the sounds of the Prayon fortress shelling the German army but we were too weary to care . . .

Chapter Twenty-four

On the morning of the 11th of May, our second day as refugees, Maman woke me up, it was barely dawn. A night on a wooden floor had not done much to rest me. As I looked at my brothers and sisters I could see that it had not done much for them either. We looked a sorry sight. Paul had the most difficulty in waking up; every time Maman sat him up, he slipped slowly down to the floor again. Papa came into the classroom carrying a pail of water he had obtained from the caretaker, and we all had a reluctant cold wash. Afterwards we had breakfast, which was a meal of bread, butter and sugar lumps.

It was intended that we would be early starters, but there were sore feet to tend and there were a few tears shed because shoes hurt. It was seven thirty before we were all set and ready for the road. What had yesterday seemed like an adventure, in the cold light of the morning became just a very sad affair. We were still tired of yesterday's walking, and now we had to walk still further! Maman tried to encourage the moaners amongst us.

"Liège is not all that far. We will be there in a few hours and once at the British Consulate our worries will be over." I don't think we all shared her optimism.

We left Prayon village school and made for the main road. Soon we were once again just another group of refugees fleeing from the advancing German hordes as if they were emanating from hell itself – as indeed they might have been, so great was our fear.

We walked on until mid-morning, when we reached the suburbs of Liège. Then on to Liège city centre and the wide boulevards. The city was teeming with people and there was chaos and confusion everywhere. Walking along beside the River

Meuse we passed a bridge which had been blown up, it lay collapsed into the water, an obscene sight offending the eyes as it spoke of the devastation and the horror of war.

We made our way to the British Consulate; planes were fighting overhead and the sound of machine-gun fire could be heard. There was one heart-stopping incident when a bullet ricocheted from the buckle on Therese's shoe then went on to break a window. We were glad to reach the Consulate and get indoors. But there, alas, disappointment awaited us, only the caretaker was left; the Consul had fled the day before. The caretaker advised us to go to the railway station from where trains were still running and try to make our way to Brussels.

Our parents were not saying very much; to walk all that way and not find help was such a blow. I felt like crying and I think my sisters felt the same. But Jean was eager to be going, Papa too. The caretaker's wife made us a cup of tea. After leaving Jean's bike at the Consulate, we found ourselves back in the streets once again. We made our way to the station; the battle in the sky was still going on but not directly overhead.

We had to cross the River Meuse on our way and we saw soldiers getting ready to blow up the bridge where we wanted to cross. They tried to stop us going on the bridge but Papa insisted that it was vital for us to get on the other side, so the soldiers told us to run as fast as we could. When we reached the station we found that trains were indeed still leaving but a terrific crowd was ranged on the platforms waiting to board them.

While we waited for a train there was a violent explosion; a huge stone came crashing through the glass roof a few feet from us. The bridge had been blown up.

After a long wait and a great deal of pushing, we eventually boarded a train. The train was packed to the roof and Papa was almost left behind at the station, but seeing our father unable to get on the train after he had successfully got the family aboard we started to scream so much that people on the platform helped Papa to get on the train through a window. After that ordeal it was with relief that we found the train making its way out of the station, then out of Liège, and we thought . . . to safety.

We had only travelled a few miles when the train came to a stop. Worried, we waited for news of the reason why we were not moving on. We soon had the answer when the roar of planes was heard, followed by the heavy thud of bomb explosions. German planes were making diving attacks on the lines. There was a general panic and many left the train to take shelter under the trees lining the embankment. Papa decided that we should stay put; with so many little ones we might become separated in the confusion. For some protection against machine-gun fire our parents stretched blankets over the carriage windows and made us lie on the floor. We lay there quietly, too frightened to move.

The attack ended but the train did not move and we spent the rest of the afternoon wondering and waiting for the train to resume its journey. We were very anxious at the lost time yet we dared not leave the train, all our hopes of getting away from the horror of the war lay with how far the train would take us and this could not be far enough.

Dusk was falling when the train eventually moved on, but we did not get very far. As it entered the small station of Ans there was another air attack. We had stopped alongside a military train and soldiers on that train were firing at the planes. It was terrifying, as if all hell was let loose. The noise of the gun fire was ear-splitting, bombs were falling all around us and there were massive explosions. We waited in the train, cowed and almost paralysed with fear.

When the planes turned away and the explosions stopped, we were given the sad news. The lines were blown up and the train could not go on. It was quite dark now, everyone left the train and with them we made our way out of the station.

We were given directions to a school but when, after walking for quite a while through what seemed a deserted town, we finally reached it, we were turned away. It was already full of refugees. We were directed to yet another school. How we found our way in the strange town in the dark night I will never know, perhaps we too have a homing instinct like Papa's pigeons which came home from all the far away places they were sent to. In the streets we walked on, making our way to a refuge for the night, we could still hear the droning of the planes and now and again there was an explosion.

Our family was very tired when we finally reached, by what I regard was nothing short of a miracle, our destination. In a large classroom straw had been laid on the floor. The classroom was crowded, full of people like ourselves running away from the war.

Willingly a place was made for us.

Another day was over; we had not gone very far but we were too tired to worry about this. We sank gratefully amongst the straw and with sleep blotting the war and our plight for a blissful few hours, we rested.

Chapter Twenty-five

Maman had hoped that we would make an early start and move out quickly from Ans but we were very lazy when morning came. The excitement and the unaccustomed exercise of the last two days was beginning to tell and it was quite a job getting the family ready for the road. Breakfast was just a few sugar lumps each, for they were all that remained in the food hamper, except for some butter.

Maman and Papa discussed our destination; Maman wanted us to make for Namur; Papa for Brussels via Waremme. Papa won and it was decided we should make for Waremme. I was hoping we would soon find some means of transport as I was awfully tired of walking. Poor little Anne and Pierre, it was harder for them. Fernand and Paul were not much bigger really; they were a tough pair those two though, never complaining.

The school was empty of refugees when we made our way out, last again! "The first thing we must do," said Maman, "is to get some food." Butter and sugar lumps couldn't sustain us for long.

We made our way to the centre of the town, and in a café we were lucky to get coffee and buns. Papa, who was wearing a three days' growth of beard, found a barber. I had been limping for a while so Maman bought me a pair of comfortable sandals. The little town of Ans was very busy that morning, with most of the shops open and doing brisk business catering for refugees.

Soon we were back on the trek again, this time feeling much fitter. We had food in our stomachs; Papa was clean shaven; my foot trouble was relieved. We made our way out of the town and soon we were in open country. Our family seemed to have left the road followed by most refugees. There were only a few people ahead of us, not the continuous file to which we had become accustomed.

We were walking really in the open now, with no trees, no hedges or protection of any kind. Suddenly, as from nowhere, the sound of machine-guns was heard. I heard the sound of an aeroplane. I looked up and, horrified, saw a plane, diving on our group.

"To the ditches!" Papa yelled.

Madeleine and Therese were walking alongside me with Anne between them holding hands. The three of us, dragging the little one, threw ourselves down the side of the road. Therese put the suitcase she was carrying on top of Anne. The four of us, terror stricken, not even knowing if the others were all right, squatted as near the ground as we could. Nearer came the plane, it passed over us, its guns spitting death. The noise receded. I looked up again; another plane had appeared and engaged the diving monster in a fight. I saw my parents, then all the boys, getting up from the ditch on the other side of the road. We ran across to each other relieved to see no one hurt. We could see a farm ahead of us and ran across the field towards it, keeping ourselves low, while the planes fought overhead. It was a dramatic situation and we were all very frightened. This was real war, and we were the target . . .

Other families had also made for the farm; we joined them in the farmyard, and all watched the battle. Then there was a roar of cheers because the battle in the sky had come to a conclusion and the Nazi plane on fire came crashing down not far from us . . . For a while we sat around getting our breath back and calming down. We were all very shaken by this ordeal and Papa decided that from now on we would avoid open spaces.

We resumed our journey to Waremme, still walking through fields, but along the hedges for protection. It was near midday on our third day as refugees and we were very hungry. We passed a deserted farm and Papa went in to look for food, reappearing carrying ten eggs. The war had not stopped the hens doing their work!

Earlier we had found a jar of jam at another deserted house. We rejoined the road and approached a house where smoke rising from the chimney spoke of an occupant.

Papa knocked on the door. The door was opened just a fraction and a woman peered at Papa. She agreed to his request to boil the eggs and took them from him, closing the door and quickly disappearing indoors. We sat around on the grass awaiting her return, as we'd already learnt to take full advantage of every spell of rest. The lady reappeared, and without a word she handed over the boiled eggs. She looked really scared and quickly shut her door on us and the rest of the world.

We found a secluded spot to sit for a meal and sat around as Maman cut the tops off the eggs. We were given an egg each and our parents shared the tops, then we had a couple of spoonfuls of jam each and a sugar lump.

If it had not been for the strangeness of our meal we might have been on a picnic, I thought. After the feast we all lay quietly resting. At that moment in time we had forgotten the war. It was very quiet and the sun shone brightly out of a cloudless sky. We were sitting under a hedge in a field near the road. The road was deserted. Therese remarked on this to Maman.

"Yes," said Maman, "I was wondering about that too." She turned to Papa. "I wonder if we are doing the right thing going to Waremme, no one else seems to be going that way."

Papa shook his head, he didn't answer. I think he was cross at having his plan questioned again. We children were enjoying our rest and it was very difficult to resume walking.

The boys dragged along, the road was uphill now, making walking harder. We walked in silence, Anne holding Maman by the hand. Pierre was having a lift on Papa's shoulders. Jean and Therese were each carrying the end of a stick passed through the handles of our suitcase and the food hamper, now also very light. I had a blanket pack slung across my shoulders; Madeleine had one too, three of the boys carried the others. We had removed our coats and Maman was carrying them over her arm. I noticed that she was limping . . . poor Maman, it was a real ordeal for her. We had gone a couple of kilometres, all uphill, when we met a group of people coming from the opposite direction. They looked curiously at us.

A man asked Papa, "Where are you making for?"

"Waremme," Papa answered.

"The Germans entered Waremme this morning, said the man, we have just left the village four kilometres from here, as the Germans entered it."

Papa went pale, he must have realised how wrong he had been

to insist on going this way and what it meant in time lost. We all were very alarmed and stood around waiting for him to speak. The other people moved on their way.

Maman spoke first.

"Come on," she said, "we must retrace our steps, it will be downhill anyway, that's come consolation."

Chapter Twenty-Six

Papa still did not speak as we all turned our backs on Waremme. We retraced our steps for a couple of kilometres, then we came to a signpost showing the way to the turn-off for Huy and soon we were well on our way. We had had a near escape, there was hope, no feared Germans had been encountered yet.

The countryside became more and more wooded and the road was now bordered by tall trees. In the heat of the afternoon the birds sang sweetly in the tree-tops. Going downhill we were making good time and we were back with the crowds again. Group after group was making its way to Huy, some people pushing loaded prams, bicycles or barrows. There were many children; sometimes an invalid in a wheelchair. It looked almost as if all Belgium had taken to the roads.

Various rumours were circulating: 'The Germans were advancing steadily,'; 'Liège was taken!' Maman told us not to listen.

"Say a prayer," she said, "that God might help us."

Late afternoon we reached an industrial area; factories were all around us. About 7 o'clock we reached a school and it was decided to call a halt for that day as we were too tired to go on. The place was crowded but there was room for us. Soon we were unpacking and settling in one of the classrooms. Papa and Jean went out to look for hot water and, if possible, food. Meanwhile Maman opened the hamper, for there was a little sugar and some butter left.

Another family was settling down in the same classroom. When they unpacked their food we saw they had plenty of bread and they were eating it dry. We did a bit of exchange with them, offering butter for a loaf of bread. Never was a loaf so welcome.

Carefully Maman halved the loaf and divided one half into twelve portions, this with sugar lumps would be our ration for tonight, the other half was put away for breakfast.

Papa and Jean returned with only a basin of hot water.

A tepid cup of tea terminated our meal. There were sore feet to bathe and tend, for some of us had huge blisters. It was still daylight when we lay down on our blankets. The other families were already settled for the night and soon there was quiet in the classroom – we fell asleep . . .

All through that long night the sound of heavy traffic could be heard on the road outside the school. Maman and Therese, awake most of the time, listened in fear, thinking that at last the German army had caught up with us. Papa went out on the road several times to see if there was any danger. There was an army on the move; tanks, gun-carriages, heavy lorries filled with soldiers were passing along the road. It was the French army moving up to take on the enemy. Moving at night gave it protection against air attacks.

In the morning we all felt the need to hurry. We were ready and on the road to Huy very early.

We arrived at Huy at eight o'clock that morning, and we decided to stop here for a short rest. The first people we met in the town were French soldiers; Papa spoke to them; they gave us a friendly handshake and when he asked to see their officer they took us to their headquarters. Maman spotted a baker's shop and managed to persuade the proprietor to let us have three loaves. These were carefully stowed away; food was an ever present and urgent problem.

At the army headquarters Maman did the talking, as Papa's French was difficult to understand. She explained our position and asked for help. They could not help and advised us to leave Huy where the French army was massing to meet the German onslaught. It was a very dejected group who travelled through that desolate city. Barely one window remained intact and the streets were littered with broken glass. Huge buildings had collapsed from bombing attacks.

Coming out of the town we had to show our identity papers to soldiers guarding special points. We took the road to Andenne. Suddenly the sound of heavy artillery filled the air, shells whistled overhead to explode a few seconds later: the fighting had begun. We hurried along; with the enemy so near we were very anxious and all thoughts of rest had gone from our minds. We must go away from what was becoming a battlefield and get as far from it as we possibly could.

Papa tried a few houses looking for a barrow to help carry the two little ones. It was a lot of walking for little legs, they were worn out and therefore slowing everyone down. In one house he found a walking stick and Maman, who was still limping, made good use of it. At midday we went into a farmyard for a rest and some food. There Papa was delighted to find a barrow at last, a heavy steel one. When we set out again Anne and Pierre were seated in it like a little king and queen in their carriage. They rather liked their new mode of transport.

We walked on with fields on one side, the River Meuse on the other. The sounds of war could still be heard. We were part of a long continuous file of fleeing people, everyone hurrying along. Our heavy barrow made a noise like a tank and people looked round to see if the dreaded enemy was in sight, greatly relieved to see it was only a barrow.

Mid-afternoon we entered a farm looking for water and were immediately ordered off the place by a soldier coming out of the house. The farm was an army headquarters and we had to move on. A few minutes later three German bombers flew overhead and one dropped something. There was a terrific explosion. It was a bomb and it had hit the farm we had just left. Panic seized the groups of refugees walking along the road. They ran in all directions; no one seemed to know quite what to do. One of the planes circled and was coming back. Papa was ahead of us, pushing the barrow with the little ones. I found myself taking shelter in the hedges with Paul and Fernand. I could see Maman and Madeleine, then Jean, David and Rene; they were all crouching in the hedges.

Three more bombs fell from the plane as it passed over and there were three more deafening explosions. We lay there watching in horror while twice again the plane circled and flew over us dropping bombs. I was praying all the time, "Please God take care of us." Heavy smoke followed the explosions and then the plane finally disappeared.

All around us was confusion, the bombs had hit the farm and the road, it was a frightening sight. Maman told us to look away from the desolate scene. Therese came running to join us; soldiers had made her go down into a cellar, she hadn't seen us during the bombing and feared for our safety. Papa, pushing his barrow with the two little ones, was walking back towards us, he was relieved to find us all safe and unhurt.

Shaking from our ordeal we moved away from the scene of devastation. I was really terrified now; what else would we have to experience? Would we always be survivors, all twelve of us? Maman was very quiet. Therese was in hysterics when she rejoined us and Maman had to calm her down. Papa had also been upset; it was obvious when he got back to us that he had feared the worst. The sheer panic amongst the refugees had been shocking to witness, but we had to go on, heading towards the big town of Namur.

In silence we walked. A couple of hours later we arrived at Andenne; we then made for Marche-les-Dames. We had another scare when a plane swooped down on our group. We all threw ourselves flat on the ground, now getting used to the attacks and reacting automatically.

Chapter Twenty-seven

We had left the River Meuse to go across country and now we rejoined it again. The view was beautiful, with mountains and hills on every side and many small craft lying at anchor on the river. We met some Belgian soldiers, one of them was from our village. He told us that Namur, where we were bound for, had been heavily bombarded all day and much of the town was on fire. But we had to go on.

We reached the outskirts of the town early that evening; the sirens were sounding an air-raid, so we had to shelter for a while. When it was safe to enter the town we were shocked at the devastation. Papa found it difficult pushing his loaded barrow because some of the pavements had huge holes. In many of the avenues there were large craters. We passed a horse lying on its side spilling its entrails onto the road. I felt sick. Buildings were just a mass of ruins, many of them on fire.

Maman hurried us along, almost running through the town, eager to be out of it. Rescues were taking place where people were possibly trapped. Ambulances stood by; everything spoke of death and devastation. For us all tiredness was forgotten; spurred on by fear we hurried on our way. Another air-raid warning sounded which made us run for shelter in a house where we huddled, listening to the heavy explosions. The family in the house advised Papa to take us to Renet just outside the town; trains were leaving from there, we might be fortunate to board one.

Half an hour later found us in Renet. Daylight was failing and we were so tired that we entered the first school we came to and settled there for the night.

At four o'clock in the morning we were woken by sirens

sounding an air-raid, so quickly we made for the cellars. Families from nearby houses joined us and some soldiers came running in from the streets. The bombing was heavy. We sat there half asleep, shivering, everyone listening nervously to the thunderous bangs and crashes. At six o'clock the all-clear sounded. We left the cellars, returning to the classroom where the younger boys lay down to go back to sleep. Papa and Jean decided to go to the railway station to enquire about trains. They returned with good news. Trains were indeed leaving for France and the first train was at nine o'clock. Very early we made our way to the station, leaving Papa and Jean to look for some food and join us later.

While we sat at the station there was another air-raid. The bombing was heavy and there were many planes. We were frightened and worried but stayed put and felt relieved, yet again, when the all-clear sounded. At nine o'clock Papa and Jean had still not returned. Maman became really anxious. A train came in and left without us. Later on another train with only two carriages came into the platform. There were a few other families waiting too, they rushed to the carriages. We were the only family left. An official came to tell us that this was the last train. Maman explained about Papa and Jean. Kindly he agreed to hold the train back for a while. Soon afterwards Papa and Jean came running into the station and hurriedly we boarded the train which left immediately.

We were so pleased that for the first time since we left our home there were smiles and jokes. It was good to feel we were getting further and further away from danger.

At Charleroi the train came to a halt, which distressed us a little as it had travelled only a few kilometres away from Namur. However, we were directed to another platform on each side of which were two long trains filling up with refugees and soon, we were told, due to leave for France. It wasn't easy to find room to accommodate our large family, and we went the length of the first train without success. At last we found an empty compartment on the second train. We settled ourselves as comfortably as possible in a compartment which was supposed to hold six. But we didn't consider this an inconvenience under the circumstances. We were thankful to be together.

The whistle blew and the train departed, we were on our way to France . . .

At Mons more refugees boarded the train; it was now very full, some people had to stand in the corridor. Tournai was our next stop where more carriages were added to our train. Suddenly an air-raid sounded, the sirens could just be heard despite the heavy droning of the planes and the noise of the bombs exploding. Everyone left the train to shelter in the station's underground. While we waited a woman gave birth to a baby. I wanted to see the baby, so did my sisters, but we could not see much as there were too many people around her. We were allowed to leave our shelter after a while and rejoined the train. We were no sooner back in our seats when the sirens wailed again. Over the loud speaker we were told to remain in the train as it was leaving. We moved out of Tournai in the thick of an air-raid; the train soon gathered speed and left it all behind.

At the end of the afternoon the train arrived at Blandin, and we refugees crossed the frontier into France. Night was falling when we entered Lille and there a nice surprise awaited us. Red Cross workers and Boy Scouts were standing by. When the train stopped they handed out food, drinks, hot milk for children and first aid if needed. That was our best meal for days. They told us that our destination was Dieppe and that we should arrive there the next day.

Settling for a night's sleep in that small compartment was not easy, there was so little room. Maman arranged us, one to lie sideways onto the other. It was a tight fit but with a bit of co-operation on our part and overwhelming tiredness, we fell asleep as soon as the train went on its way.

Chapter Twenty-eight

I woke on the morning of the 15th May to find the train had stopped at a station and Red Cross personnel were bringing breakfast to the refugees.

Our parents had not slept all night because we kept falling off the seats, and they had decided to watch over us. There had been air-raids during the night, and the train had stopped at sidings for long periods. We had slept on, relaxing after our ordeals. For our parents it had been an exhausting night.

When the train finally resumed its journey we gave Maman a whole seat so that she could have a good rest. Papa decided to lie on the floor between the seats where he promptly fell asleep; his feet were sticking into the corridor and as we were the last compartment near the toilet everyone had to step over him, but he slept on . . .

The train carried on its journey, stopping at times for long periods, then again at large stations where refreshments were handed to us. We were allowed to stretch our legs a bit although there were always soldiers patrolling the platforms and we were not allowed to move very far. However, everything we needed was brought to us so this did not worry us.

We heard that our train was the eighteenth train full of refugees making its way through France. We were glad to hear that so many had escaped like us. It was a lovely feeling being on a train speeding away from the horrors of war. We had been told that we were on our way to Dieppe, Papa hoped that we would be able to get a ship from there and sail to England. The train took all day to reach Dieppe. Papa called it jokingly the 'milk train' for it stopped so often and travelled slowly. My father had travelled more than I ever had, a train moving was a train speeding to me.

It was dark when we reached Dieppe and there was a heavy thunderstorm over the town. Large flashes of lightning streaked brightly in the dark sky. Therese was very frightened, I wasn't to reassured either; after all, trains are made of steel and I remembered what Maman had always said about steel being a good conductor of electricity. I hoped that after having come through so much we would not die through being struck by lightning.

The train stopped at Dieppe and Papa was allowed to go and see the Station Master to ask if we could leave the train. Meanwhile we were fed for the last time that day, and we heard that another night must be spent on the train by the refugees as the train had to move on from Dieppe. Papa returned to tell us that we were not allowed to leave the train, the chances of getting on a ship at Dieppe were not good; we too must travel on.

A few sick refugees left us that evening and were taken by ambulances to hospital. Maman's foot was pretty bad, red and inflamed, but she would not mention it to the nurses in case they took her to hospital too.

The train left Dieppe and once again we settled for another night's sleep, one lying against the other. When morning came our third day on the train started like the previous day; breakfast was brought to us and then we went on our way; the train, we were told, making its way to Poitiers.

We were getting restless. Travelling on and on had been interesting at first but to spend a third day in the crowded conditions we were in wasn't an exciting prospect, however we were getting away from the war and surely we must stop somewhere. The boys spent most of the time in the corridor, I mostly sat looking out of the window with Anne on my knees. Some of us had swollen ankles now and Maman's foot was no better. With Papa she had spent another night awake, so as we travelled on they both slept.

Our meals were served as the previous day, and once again we had very long stops at sidings; probably waiting for lines to clear, Papa had explained. Of our fellow travellers we took very little notice. I don't think anyone was in a mood for much conversation.

Once, at a stop, we watched soldiers escorting a man, handcuffed, away to the back of the train and the whispers going around were that the man was a fifth columnist. I had heard that word mentioned more than once during our ordeals and knew its meaning. The man would probably be shot. Even on the train carrying us to safety there was danger.

We passed through Le-Mans, and as night fell we reached Poitiers. There were still no signs of reaching our destination that day so we settled for another night. We were still not sure where we were heading.

On the fourth day on the train my legs were very swollen, as were Therese's, Jean's and Madeleine's. We were told after a meal early that morning that Bordeaux was our destination. On our way to that town the countryside became outstandingly beautiful and to my great joy we saw the sea. It was the first time in my life that I had seen the sea. I had always been envious of my school friends who had holidays by the seaside and now I too had seen the sea and soon would probably sail on it. Then I remembered the U-boats which now lay in wait for ships to sink and I wished that Papa would abandon all thoughts of going to England; it was too dangerous.

We passed Bordeaux, and still we travelled on! At ten o'clock that evening the train stopped and we were allowed to get out and go for refreshments. This was the first time we had been allowed to leave the train other than to stretch our legs. Papa decided to go but he was soon back, afraid perhaps that the train might leave without him. The boys were still asleep. I had toothache and felt miserable. A Red Cross nurse moving along the corridor told us to try and stay awake because we would soon reach our destination.

The train moved on and I fell asleep. Maman shook me awake, saying, "Get ready, we have arrived."

It was about midnight when our sleepy group climbed off the train which had been our home for the last four days. We followed the crowd of refugees and walked out of the station. No one seemed to know where we were and no one seemed to care either. Maman was limping badly, Papa was carrying Anne, Therese and I were helping Pierre and Fernand, the others followed, everyone was half asleep.

We came to a large square where buses, cars, horses and carts were parked. There were many people waiting in the square. We had been told to form a queue. As we slowly moved forwards, I heard a voice shout, "A family of five," then "A family of three, over here." The two family groups moved forward, they got into cars and were driven away. The queue slowly moved up, after a while it was our turn. Someone shouted:

"A family of twelve," – there was a pause, then a huge man stepped forwards:

"I'll take them." With a sweeping gesture of his hand he made a sign, slowly a bus drew up. With the help of the big man we boarded it. I heard a small man who hovered in the shadow of the big one saying:

"Monsieur le Baron, there is room left."

Monsieur le Baron collected more families to fill the bus. In our turn we were driven away. It was dark and nothing could be seen as we drove on for quite a way. We could see the headlights of a car following us; Monsieur le Baron was seeing his protégées to their new home.

The bus came to a halt. Peering through the windows I could see a crowd of people, some carrying candles, coming forwards to greet us. Slowly the bus emptied. Papa was in front of me carrying Anne who was fast asleep. From the waiting crowd hands were stretched to take her. Madeleine and I kept close to each other, then I felt Paul's hand slide into mine. Therese was helping Maman who had difficulty in walking. I could see in the darkness a huge building; a woman said to me, "It's a presbytery."

We all entered the house, following the candle-bearing woman into a large room. There seemed to be food everywhere, the large table in the middle of the room was covered with food of all kinds. Maman told the woman that sleep was all we needed at the moment and we were led upstairs, distributing ourselves into four bedrooms. Bunk beds were the only furniture.

Then the woman left us to sort ourselves out, and before long we were all fast asleep – still not knowing where in France we were.

Chapter Twenty-Nine

The train which had brought us down to the South of France had done so many detours that once we finally stepped off it we were completely disorientated. We had no clear idea where exactly we were now domiciled. In the morning after our arrival we first took stock of the house and its surroundings and of our fellow refugees.

The house where we had spent our first night as refugees on French soil was a large presbytery which had seen better days. We shared it with another family; a man, his wife and their little daughter and the lady's sister. In the morning we all met downstairs in the large living-room.

The previous night when we had entered the house we had found it full of all kinds of food, that morning we ate what had so kindly been prepared for us. We ate boiled eggs, salads, cold ham and potatoes. In fact the first day no cooking was necessary, there was so much cooked food available.

The actual cooking facilities at the house were primitive; an ancient wood fire was to both heat the room and cook our food. Maman decided that she would feed the family on soups and stews and that the most important cooking implement we must acquire was a large cooking pot. On our quest as to how and where we could obtain the cooking pot we stepped outside our new home and set out to meet the inhabitants of the hamlet of La Jalabertie.

La Jalabertie, a tiny hamlet, near Toulouse in the South of France, had the inhabitants of a dozen farms as its only population. They made a living from the land; vineyards and potato fields were all around. Monsieur le Baron, who had an old castle in a little town some miles away, did all the administration in the area. Dominating the small hamlet was the small church and presbytery, and an avenue of trees, where a well which we would depend on for water was situated, led to these buildings.

Stepping outside the house we found ourselves in a world of sunshine, country air and trees. There was another large building near us. Three families had found rooms there. We had much in common with them; we all had lost our homes and our possessions, and we all felt very strange in these new surroundings. We three girls, with Maman, introduced ourselves to our neighbours. We felt very friendly towards each other; forgetting the cooking-pot, for the best part of the morning we talked about our war experiences.

One lady, Madame Martin, who had escaped with her husband, was very distressed. Another lady, Madame Leman, who had escaped with her daughter Micheline, was trying very hard to ease the sorrows of Madame Martin by assuring her that we would very soon return to our home, but Madame Martin was so upset that all we could get from her were constant cries for a good cup of coffee – it was amazing at a time like this what people clung to. We had no coffee at that moment so all that was offered was wine which the farmers had supplied us with in plenty. Then there was Misha and her husband Sacha, they introduced themselves; they were a young polish couple, both doctors, who spoke very little about themselves. During our stay at La Jalabertie they were unfailingly friendly but kept their air of mystery for they never revealed their surname.

After the long and difficult journey we had done, there was something very peaceful and welcoming at La Jalabertie. We walked around in the soft, relaxing air of the morning. Down a small lane at the back of the house we came to two houses; one of them a farm. When the inhabitants saw us they immediately came out of their houses to ask how we had slept and if we had any immediate needs. Shops, we learned, were a long way off in the small market town of Revel, about six kilometres away. We learned that the baker called daily and that we could buy eggs, milk and wine from the farm and even some vegetables.

We had a very personal worry; this was almost a total lack of money. That afternoon Monsieur le Baron called on us and we were given money. The French authorities made a daily allowance to the refugees regardless of personal circumstances.

The appearance of Monsieur le Baron was a great relief to our parents. We also learned that we were expected to stay put. Because there were large numbers of refugees in the South of France and many families were separated, the task of bringing order to the present chaos would be lessened if everyone registered in one area. Lists of the names of those seeking relatives could be seen at the Town Hall in Revel.

The farmers of the small hamlet went shopping once a week at Revel; to reach the town they cycled. They were pleased to lend a bicycle to anyone wishing to make the trip. Papa, for some reason, preferred to walk. With Jean he departed the following day for the town of Revel, with a shopping list and our now empty hamper. It was quite some time before they returned. They brought back a large, bright red, cooking pot, ideal for cooking soups and stews for the twelve of us. The boys were given the task of seeking firewood. The farmers were generous for, at times, it was wood cut ready for the fire that the boys brought home.

One very important happening every morning at La Jalabertie was the arrival of the postman. He was also a newspaper seller. Our news of the war and its progress came to us via the postman. Daily the news grew worse. Our elders would stand every day, after the arrival of the post, gathered at the well to learn how the German army was advancing and conquering. First it was Belgium, the day of the capitulation of our country bringing great sorrow for us. Towns were invaded and we learned that Paris was declared an open city.

We who had hoped to return to our homes very soon, took all this news with great distress, so the much awaited arrival of the postman brought only consternation and sadness.

Maman and Papa would go indoors with their newspapers, the little group beside the well would disperse. But we young ones would soon forget the news as we decided how to spend another day of what was like a holiday. For at La Jalabertie, despite what the newspapers said, there was only peace and sunshine.

The farmers were very busy with much cultivation taking place; the vines were growing fruits and had to be tended and sprayed, and the potato crops had the same treatment for the dreaded colorado beetle was in residence. Daily we went to the fields with the farmer and his daughter Denise. The boys soon made friends with the farmers too, and as we passed along the road of La Jalabertie, Madeleine and I, with Micheline, we saw David and Rene, Jean and Paul, in farmers' fields or yards busy at some job or other. I don't know how much help we were really, but the farmers made us welcome and in the evenings we shared the large meal they ate when the work of the day was over.

Irene and Denise were the only two young girls who were resident in La Jalabertie, so to them the arrival of refugees must have brought quite a diversion in their peaceful life. We were soon great friends with them and when they could leave their daily tasks they took us for walks around the countryside. We lived at the foot of the Pyrenees, or it seemed like that anyway. There were many wooded areas around and a fast flowing river was not too far away. We liked going there to bathe our feet in the water which, coming from the mountains, was icy cold. It was June and the weather was very hot, so we spent many hours by that river.

There was another small river, not too far away, where we went fishing with a very elementary rod and a piece of string to which we tied a worm. We soon learned that it was no use bringing the fish home. Papa could not stand the sight of fish freshly taken from the river where he declared emphatically, "They were so happy." One day we had brought home a pail full of small fishes meant for the next day, which was a Friday. Papa made such a fuss about "the poor little fishes" that we took them back to the river and threw them into the water where they swam away unaware that they had escaped being in the frying pan because of the soft heart of an Englishman. Another day a farmer gave us a chicken, once again Papa was adamant – no fish, no fowl. We saw the chicken being given to Madame Leman and Micheline who made a feast out of it.

Living as we did a lot of the niceties of life had to be dispensed with. There was no tablecloth, no saucers and very little cutlery. We did not worry, for it meant very little housework; few dishes to wash, few clothes to clean. Although not everyone felt as we did. Madame Leman found it hard to accept a rustic way of life and went to a great deal of trouble to preserve some degree of decorum. However, Micheline was a very modern girl, very resourceful, quite a contrast to her gentle 'decorum loving' mother, who she was always shocking. Micheline trapped pigeons, killed them and presented them to her mother to supplement their diet. Forgiving her daughter's audacity, Madame Leman cleaned and cooked the pigeons; she put vegetables in the cooking pot and put the pan on the ancient fire, where she took turns at cooking with the other two families. There ended the rustic part of the meal because once the pan was off the fire, she would begin the 'ritual' of serving the meal. First the liquid part of the cooked stew was put on a plate to be called 'the soup', when this was eaten Madame Leman would fish out the vegetables and this would be the 'entree'. Finally the potatoes and pigeon would take their place on the plate; this being the main part of the dinner. Micheline laughingly told us about her properly served dinner. But when we had laughed about all the fancy arrangements we would shake our heads, "Poor Madame Leman," we declared, "she does miss her home!"

Micheline's father was lost, they had become separated during the escape from Belgium and had not yet been able to locate each other – poor Madame Leman she had a lot of worries . . .

On the first Sunday of our stay at La Jalabertie, the church was opened by Irene whose task it was to keep the church cleaned and ready for the Sunday services.

A priest arrived from the town of Revel to say Holy Mass and inhabitants from areas around the hamlet came to take part in the service. During the sermon the priest, on behalf of himself and the congregation, gave a warm welcome to the refugees, wishing them a happy stay in the area and a swift return to their homes.

After the Mass ended and the church was once again closed, the congregation returned to their respective homes and La Jalabertie was once again as quiet and as undisturbed as if nothing had taken place. One of the feelings one had at the small hamlet was that of isolation, of being far away from the world of shops, cars and trains, industries and people. Our village of Andrimont was a hive of activity by comparison.

In the evenings, which were already long and summery, we would go to the bottom of the lane. With Irene, Denise and their parents we would congregate. Maman would walk over and we would pass the time of day. It was a very peaceful time and the horrors of war seemed remote as we talked of better days.

Papa was happy under the circumstances, for he had discovered that the wine made by the farmers, besides being very good to drink, was also very cheap! He had acquired a taste for it. He had a lot of worries – no job, no home, nothing to do but wait for an end to the hostilities – so he did his best to drown all his sorrows. Whenever he was seen, he had a bottle of wine bulging out of his pocket; he had problems and he could do very little about our present situation, the wine helped him to forget.

We had no idea how long our present circumstances would last. For the summer Maman was quite content with the present arrangements, for the winter it would be more difficult; the beds we slept on were rudimentary – they had straw mattresses and pillows but there was no bed linen and only two blankets per bed. The house wasn't heated upstairs so we would not be warm enough. The sum of money we were allocated each week was modest but adequate for our present food and fuel cost, and we were able to buy odds and ends like sandals and kitchen implements. Maman was trying very hard to save some of the money for the winter's needs but each week she found herself awaiting Monsieur le Baron's visit, and so was everyone else.

Monsieur le Baron arrived once a week driven in an ancient car by a small man with small sharp black eyes, unfailingly wearing a beret in the basque fashion. The small man's respect for his master was evident as he tried to anticipate his master's every move. Monsieur le Baron was a huge man dressed in tweeds. He had a gruff voice and manners to match. Despite the gruff voice his manner to us was that of a benevolent Santa Claus. He carried, slung across his shoulder, a large money bag. At his arrival, which could never have gone unnoticed as the old car clunk-clunked its way along the road, everyone came out to meet him. After having given us the latest news concerning the war – which he delivered almost like a lecture – he would proceed to distribute his bounty, kindly provided by the French authorities. The money was easily divided, with each adult receiving the same amount, each child ditto. His task achieved, Monsieur le Baron would grandly bow to everyone and remount his battered car.

We were rich once again and Maman would go indoors to plan her budget with great care. Poor Maman, it wasn't an easy task for her, there were so many things which we needed. Her foot had caused many worries. It had turned septic and she refused to see a doctor. Therese had bathed the injured foot with devotion and one day we were all thankful to learn that the foot was healing.

We young ones settled very well. This was the first time that we had spent some time away from home, so it was like a holiday and we fully enjoyed it. We were thankful that we had survived the fearful days, not at all anxious as to what lay ahead, in some ways living in a fool's paradise. Probably our mind's reaction was to shut out all that we had experienced, or else the peaceful countryside was such an extreme from what we had left behind – the bombing, the machine-gunning, the frightened people, the dead – that like a balm our peaceful existence calmed all our fears and worries.

A couple of weeks went by and the weather was superb in mid-June. Life in the area where we were was back to normal. The refugees had been accepted with kindness by the inhabitants of La Jalabertie. We felt as if we had been part of their lives for a long time. Anne, Pierre and Fernand played mostly around the presbytery. Pierre was an inventive child who kept the other two amused with his made-up games. Maman sat outside in the sun, mostly sewing to repair our meagre wardrobe. We were on our own at the presbytery now, the other family having moved away to a small cottage to be near some relatives. It meant that Maman could relax completely, allowing the young ones to make as much noise as normal youngsters make.

It was to Madeleine and I that the task of doing the weekly wash fell. We washed the clothes in a small river at the back of the presbytery, which was for us a novel way of doing things. We simply threw all the clothes in the water with the soap, then we sat around in the sun letting the gentle flow of the water clean the clothes. It was the best washing machine ever invented and certainly the pleasantest way of doing that chore.

While we waited peacefully in the South of France for our return to Belgium the war situation was worsening. In our early days in La Jalabertie, Papa had informed the Consulate in Bordeaux of our whereabouts. One day a telegram arrived from the Consulate requesting 'Your presence in Bordeaux', it was addressed to Papa only. Alas, when Papa arrived in Bordeaux he found that it was the whole family for whom the message was meant. A ship was due to sail in two day's time for England and in view of the worsening war conditions we were to sail on it.

Papa returned by the next train. He arrived back at the presbytery in the evening with the news that we would leave for

Bordeaux the following day. As a family we were thrown into a state of consternation. We wanted to go home, not further away. Going to England was something we all wanted to do at some time in our lives, but not as refugees. If we had to leave La Jalabertie could it not be for our village? There would be no fighting there any more. Papa reminded us that we would immediately be arrested and no doubt interned.

I was adamant that I wasn't going to England and begged Maman to leave me with the farmers. I was afraid to cross the sea, afraid of the submarines, the planes, the mines. I had an awful feeling of dread that if we sailed on that ship we would never reach England. In view of the fact that we only had a few hours to arrange our departure Maman was patient with me and those who felt like me. Seeing the level way she took this new upheaval we felt ashamed of giving her more worry, and after a while we were all sorting out our meagre belongings and making arrangements for the next day when we had to catch an early bus for Toulouse on the first part of the journey.

Then we settled to spend our last night at the house which had been our refuge for the last four weeks. We were very sad. This was going to be good-bye forever. One day we would go back home, but the likelihood of coming back to this remote part of France seemed negligible.

The following day all those we knew assembled by the well to say their good-byes, we would write and keep in touch . . . Micheline, losing two friends, was trying to be cheerful. There wasn't much future for Micheline, she disappeared in the terrible concentration camps a few years later. We, who were about to cross the Bay of Biscay, were the ones at that moment who looked as if the future was in doubt . . .

So we said good-byes to all those who had shared our experiences as refugees and soon we were on our way once again.

Chapter Thirty

It was the morning of the 21st of June that we left La Jalabertie on our way to the town of Toulouse. On arrival at the town we made our way to the station. There we met our first difficulty; we did not have enough money to pay for our train journey to Bordeaux. At the station Papa showed his passport and Maman explained our position, telling the ticket officer that we were an English family making our way to Bordeaux to embark on a ship for repatriation.

The man in the booking office was adamant; no money, no tickets! We children stood around hopefully, awaiting an amicable settlement to the argument. Maman, seeing that she was making no impression on the ticket officer, asked to see the Station Master. Leaving us with Papa and taking Therese along with her she followed a station employee.

They were away for some time before finally returning — Maman was triumphant. She told us how the Station Master, probably mellowed by Therese's tears, had said on hearing our story: "Madame, if this should cost me my job, ticket or no ticket, your family will get to Bordeaux."

He gave the orders for the ticket collector to admit our family to the platform. All smiles, we sat patiently awaiting our train.

The station was quite busy and sitting there we watched all the comings and goings. An old lady was pacing the platform, wheeling a push-chair on which there were two rabbits in a cage then another cage containing a cat, on top of these there was still another cage containing pigeons. I wondered where the poor old lady was going with her menagerie, but I must say that I felt really sorry for the child holding on to the push-chair in which he should have been sitting!

Soon we were once again on a train, this time on our way to England. It seemed like yesterday that we had journeyed not knowing our destination; then it had been La Jalabertie and a very happy time spent there, now it was the unknown again, an unknown called England where people spoke a language which we did not understand. For sixteen years I had lived in a small village, dreaming sometimes of travelling to far away lands, but not in my wildest dreams had I imagined journeys like these, made in uncertainty and fear; for we must now cross the sea with its hidden dangers, a sea made frightening by war. I heard Madeleine ask Maman, "What will we do if a submarine attacks the boat?"

"Sh . . . you must not think like that," said Maman, who was obviously anxious that her family should stay calm.

We arrived in Bordeaux that evening. Night had fallen so there was no question of joining the ship in the dark.

"Better wait until morning," said Papa.

We sat in a waiting-room at the station; we would have to spend the night there as our finances did not run to hotel accommodation. A station official came into the waiting-room and asked if we had anywhere to spend the night. Maman told him what we proposed to do.

"Go to the end of the platform where the group of people are waiting," was his advice.

We joined the group and we were told that we would be taken to a warehouse where we could spend the night.

We reached the warehouse after a walk through dark streets and there in its large rooms we settled ourselves, once again sleeping on the floor amongst fellow travellers.

We were awakened during the night by the sound of explosions – Maman said softly, "There is an air-raid on. Don't be afraid, it will soon be over."

Therese, Madeleine and Jean were also awake. We were in an upstairs room. The explosions seemed to be coming nearer and nearer and we could hear the droning of planes. Some people made their way downstairs in the dark, but one man lit a match so he could see his way; there was an uproar and the light went out immediately. The boys were waking up; Anne and Pierre were crying. The bombing went on and a bomb fell so close that the building shook. Someone screamed and started banging the big warehouse door. There was sudden panic as we realised we had been locked in the warehouse by the station officials. We were like mice in a trap.

Some of the men tried to ram the huge doors but with so little success that at last they gave up. We had no further sleep that night. The bombing went on until dawn. When the doors were finally unlocked, lack of sleep and the fearful night we had spent made us look haggard in the morning light.

The little ones were fretful; Papa was carrying Pierre who was feverish. Maman, as usual, was her courageous self. "Let's cheer up," said said, "we are still alive, soon we will be on the ship and then in England, then all will be well."

We stopped at the station for coffee and sandwiches and then we made our way to the docks. But when we arrived there was no large ship in sight anywhere. The docks, in fact, looked deserted. We walked on, passing wharf after wharf. Papa asked a man who was busy rolling large coils of rope if he knew of a ship due to leave for England that day.

"Yes," replied the man, "it was lying there yesterday." He pointed to a wharf, then added: "It left last night during the air-raid to avoid the bombing."

We looked stupidly to where the ship should have been lying, unable to believe that it was well and truly gone.

Our parents looked lost for words. I think they couldn't imagine what to do next. We moved away sadly and for a while we wandered aimlessly through the town.

The ship had gone. There we were in Bordeaux, miles away from home, with very little money, no prospect of a home of any kind; a family lost and desolate. We did not even speak to each other. At that awful moment I desperately longed for the security of Andrimont; our house, our friends and all that we had left. It would be so nice to go back in time and have it all back just the way it was. I could see in Maman's face that she too felt really desperate, with all the young children following her sadly awaiting a decision from her as to what we were going to do now. It was Papa who spoke, "Let's find the Consulate."

It was not just a ray of hope. To me it was like a flash of genius; the Consulate, of course there was the Consulate, we would find help there.

We were directed to it by a passer-by, but when we finally

reached it, we were told by the caretaker that no one was on the premises.

Nevertheless we felt a bit cheered by the sight of other British families in the same predicament as ourselves. They, too, had turned up at the Consulate seeking help. Someone suggested that we should go to the American Consulate.

We made our way through the unfamiliar streets and boulevards. Arriving at the American Consulate, Maman made us sit on the stairs until it was our turn to see the Consul. We waited a long time; a woman fainted; someone had hysterics. Then a tall man appeared at one of the doors and asked if there were British people present. Judging by the answers we were fairly numerous – the man added, "You must seek help from your own Consul, he is still in Bordeaux."

Calling the next Americans waiting into his room, he closed the door. There were some British soldiers waiting and already Papa had made friends with them. Together we made our way back to the British Consulate. The doors of the Consulate were now opened but the caretaker still denied the presence of the Consul on the premises. Some of the people were very angry and voices were raised.

We waited outside sitting on our luggage. So far that day we had only eaten a few sandwiches. Papa decided to go into the town to seek food, but he had not been away long when a lorry drove up and all the British families were told to get on it. The lorry was on its way to Bayonne where a ship was leaving for England the following day.

Maman was frantic, possibly our last chance and Papa was away. The driver refused to wait; soon we were the only ones left in front of the Consulate.

Maman was crying and so were all we girls; the boys watched us forlornly. Anne put her little arms around Maman's neck to try and comfort her. Then a soldier came out of the Consulate and seeing our desolate group told us not to worry too much – the Consul was still there, we would be helped somehow.

Papa returned with a few oranges which were all that he had found as shops were closed everywhere. When he was told about the lorry he nearly broke down himself.

We waited all the afternoon, and other families joined us; by evening we were nearly forty. We had almost given up hope of anything being done for us that day when a limousine drove up in front of the Consulate. A French officer got out of the car and entered the building. He reappeared with an English officer whom we were told was the Consul. When he moved towards the car some of the men stepped in his path. The Consul told the crowd that he was going to arrange with the French authorities for transport to Bayonne for all of us. Only when he agreed to take two men from the crowd with him was he allowed to leave.

And so we waited . . . until a large bus drove up. We were told that a train would take all British families to Bayonne where a ship was due to sail for England. The bus took us to the railway station where we were told to keep together in a waiting-room while we waited for the train.

We were tired and hungry and when the Red Cross opened a canteen at the station we were very grateful for the refreshments.

At nearly two o'clock in the morning our train finally came in. The youngest children were fast asleep already and had to be carried into the carriage. There was plenty of room so we made ourselves comfortable and were soon all fast asleep.

I woke up early next morning as the train entered Bayonne's station. Helping the younger ones with their dressing was easy because we had not done much undressing the night before. We were met by a station official who told us to form a line. In that long line we came out of the station, walked through the town and made our way to the docks.

We halted in front of the customs buildings, and there we waited – standing around at first, then as morning wore on we spread around and settled on the grass verges. Our biggest worry was food, or rather lack of it. Other families unpacked sandwiches, cakes and biscuits, and we just looked on. Papa and Jean, once again, went looking for something to eat. When they returned Jean had received from a kind French lady, from whom he had asked what the possibilities of obtaining food were, a bag of sugar lumps and two tins of sardines. Papa had only obtained five small cakes. We shared the food. We were used to strange meals by now!

Papa had also been news gathering. The latest was that the German army was advancing steadily through France, the French government was in Bordeaux. Everywhere was chaos. Listening to Papa I felt it would be so good to get away from it all.

In front of our little picnic site was the river, but nowhere could we see a ship large enough to take our crowd. Towards four o'clock the customs doors were opened and we took our place in the queue. Papa had some difficulty convincing the officials that we were all one family; his passport was on his name only and Maman did not possess one. I felt a moment of panic; what if we were not able to board the ship? But all was well, we were waved on.

She was there all right; we came upon her round the bend of the river. A Dutch liner called *Koningin Emma*. She seemed big to me, who had never seen a liner before, but according to Papa she was only of modest size.

We waited with the crowd as some soldiers who had befriended us boarded first. Suddenly, through the megaphone, the voice of the officer in charge at the gangway boomed:

"Make way please for Mr and Mrs Docherty and their ten children."

I think our soldier friends were responsible for this. As we moved forwards up the gangway the soldiers formed like a guard of honour and patted our heads as we passed.

We left French soil early that evening amid good-byes and the singing of *La Marseillaise*. A large crowd of French people waved the ship away. There were tears in our eyes and there was hope in our hearts, the end of the journey was in sight.

"Thank you God," I said from the bottom of my heart, "please let this ship cross the sea safely under your care."

The voyage was not uneventful. We were chased by a U-boat until our SOS brought British ships to escort us. We reached Plymouth harbour on the evening of June 24th – six and a half weeks after leaving our little Belgian village of Andrimont. As the ship prepared to anchor in Plymouth, the boys were jumping for joy.

Maman looked relieved as she hugged Anne. Papa kept repeating proudly, "This is England."

Yes indeed, this was England . . . where Papa had told us in the past that the "Water's like Champagne". There was no doubt how he felt about his country. It would be good to step ashore and see Papa's land.

But all that really mattered now was that we were safe. The future could take care of itself.

As for the 'House of David', as it was known in Andrimont, it would be there for us when the war ended. One day we would go back. Maman had already decided that we would not sell it; we could not stand losing it twice.

With that hope in my heart I gave a sigh of relief and removed my life jacket, then looking around at my family and giving a hug to Madeleine, I gave a silent prayer of thanks.

Epilogue

We arrived at Plymouth on the 25th June 1940. There we disembarked and we went through customs to where a buffet had been prepared for us. We ate well for we were starving. The young people all received a packet of biscuits and some chocolate as we were led out of the customs to board a long train for London.

In London the train was met by a fleet of buses which took us across the city to a theatre named the 'Empress Hall'. There awaiting us was a well laid dinner. Afterwards we were handed carbolic soap and a towel and joined a file waiting to take a bath, males at one side and females at the other. Papa, who had many relatives in London, left us in the afternoon to go and visit them. He returned later accompanied by his brother and soon we too were on our way to meet Papa's relatives, where a great welcome awaited us.

In the evening we found ourselves distributed around different areas of London to spend the night with relatives.

We stayed in London for two days, where the children enjoyed a trip to the zoo and the girls were entertained by our English cousins whose welcome warmed our hearts.

We had been issued with a free travel permit on our arrival at the Empress Hall. After two days in London we left for Hebburn, a small town on Tyneside, and there we 'invaded' the home of my father's sister and her family. To accommodate twelve people is not easy but they did their best. I did see my dear little aunt wiping tears from her eyes and I did wonder why at the time. Food was already in very short supply with most things on ration.

Papa celebrated his homecoming, Hebburn being his boyhood home, renewing old friendships.

He was fortunate to find a job, though sadly with a small wage. We needed money sorely as our French money had no value in England because of the war. Only a very small house was available to rent. Eight days after our arrival in Hebburn my family, pushing a little borrowed cart on which was perched two mattresses, a table, a chest of drawers and sundry small items, left our kind relatives to make our way to our new 'domain'.

A quarter of an hour later we entered our new home. A shabby old house with gas-lighting, outside cold water tap and toilet. Our 'bits and pieces' did not take long to unload. Maman, seeing her young daughters sad faces, said gently, "We can clean this place." I felt we were imprisoned; but no, we were free and safe. We had to bear that in mind as we settled down to await the end of the war and our return to Andrimont.

In the years we spent in that house, problem after problem faced us. It was Maman who somehow solved our health and well-being difficulties. To us Maman was a saint. She taught us to laugh at the twists and turns of life. If she shed tears she never showed them.

Eventually the younger ones went to school, the older children found work, war work I must add. John (Jean) went away to Canada with the RAF to train as a pilot, to be later involved in the Berlin air lift and troubles in Palestine.

Then we received the biggest blow of all; Maman was suffering from cancer. We lost her after a two year struggle to get her well again. Desolation fell on our family. Our house in Belgium was sold and the only thoughts of going back to Belgium were to spend a holiday there. As the years passed we became the pilgrims of Andrimont as many family trips were arranged.

A small shrine has been erected by the priest of the Church of St. Laurent in Andrimont. It is on the roadside facing our house. It is a mark of thanksgiving to those who endured so much tragedy due to the war and for my family's escape.

Life moved on . . . the war clouds lifted and there started the rebuilding of shattered lives, the rebuilding of towns and cities. Every one of the ten children eventually married and had families of their own.

Papa went to join Maman. Aptly for an old soldier he left this world on the 11th November 1953. We watched at his graveside as the tributes were given to him by his old comrades of the British Legion; one by one they filed past his coffin and dropped red poppies into his grave, Papa was an Englishman through and through.

L-R: MARGUERITE, ANNE, MARIE-THERESE, MARIE-MADELEINE